Princeton Theological Monograph Series

Dikran Y. Hadidian

General Editor

15

The Tondrakian Movement

Religious Movements in the Armenian Church
from the fourth to the tenth centuries

The Tondrakian Movement

Religious movements in the Armenian church from the fourth to the tenth centuries

Vrej Nersessian

PICKWICK *Publications* • Eugene, Oregon

Pickwick Publications
An imprint of Wipf and Stock Publishers
199 W 8th Ave, Suite 3
Eugene, OR 97401

The Tondrakian Movement
Religious movements in the Armenian church from the fourth to the tenth centuries
By Nersessian, Vrej

ISBN 13: 978-0-915138-99-9
ISBN 10: 0-915138-99-9
Publication date 1/1/1988
Previously published by Kahn & Averill, 1987

Dedicated to
HIS HOLINESS VAZGEN I Catholicos of All the Armenians on the occasion of His 30th anniversary of enthronement
30th September, 1955

CONTENTS

ABBREVIATIONS

ARB–BL	*Académie Royale de Belgique, Bulletin Classe des Lettres*
B	*Byzantion,* (Brussels)
BGA	*Bibliotheca geographorum arabicorum,* M. J. de Goeje, ed. (Leyden)
BK	*Bedi Kartlisa* (Paris)
BL	*Book of Letters* (Tiflis, 1901)
BM	*Banber Matenadarani* (Erevan)
BS	*Byzantinoslavica* (Prague)
BSOAS	*Bulletin of the School of Oriental and African Studies* (London)
BZ	*Byzantinische Zeitschrift* (Munich)
CHA	*Collection des Historiens Arméniens,* M. Brosset (St. Petersburg, 1876)
CHAMA	*Collection des Historiens anciens et modernes de l'Arménie,* V. Langlois (Paris, 1868 - 1869)
CMH	*Cambridge Medieval History* (Cambridge)
CSCO	*Corpus Scriptorum Christianorum Orientalium* (Louvain)
CSHB	*Corpus Scriptorum Historiae Byzantinae* (Bonn, 1828 - 1897)
DAI	*De Administrando Imperio,* G. Moravcsik, R. J. H. Jenkins, et al, ed., and trans. (Budapest - London, 1949, 1962)
DOP	*Dumbarton Oaks Papers* (Cambridge, Mass. and Washington)
ECQ	*Eastern Churches Quarterly* (Ramsgate)
EHR	*English Historical Review* (London)
EO	*Echos d'Orient* (Constantinople and Paris, 1827 - 1942. Cont. as *B*)
HA	*Handēs Amsoryeay* (Vienna)
HTR	*Harvard Theological Review* (Cambridge, Mass.)
IANA	*Izvestia Akademii Nauk Armianskoi SSR* (Erevan)
JA	*Journal Asiatique* (Paris)
JAOS	*Journal of the American Oriental Society* (Baltimore)
JHS	*Journal of Hellenic Studies* (London)
JRAS	*Journal of the Royal Asiatic Society* (London)
KT	*The Key of Truth,* F. C. Conybeare, ed.
MW	*Muslim World* (London)
OCP	*Orientalia Christiana Periodica* (Rome)
PBH	*Patma-Banasirakan Handes* (Erevan)
PG	*Patrologiae cursus completus.* Series graeco-latina, J. P. Migne, ed. (Paris, 1857 - 1866)
REA	*Revue des Études Arméniennes* (Paris)
T	*Teɫekagir* see *IANA*
VV	*Vizantiĭski Vremennik* (Moscow)
ZKG	*Zeitschrift für Kirchengeschichte* (Tübingen und Gotha)

INTRODUCTION

The origin of Christianity in Armenia has always been a matter of acute controversy. This is not surprising for there was no literature in the Armenian language during the first four centuries and therefore we have no contemporary written document concerning the beginning of Christianity in Armenia. All the writings on this subject date from the fifth century. What is relevant to our purpose is that the rapid advance of the Christian faith in Armenia in the second and third centuries paved the way for national acceptance of Christianity as the official religion at the end of the third (A.D. 287 or 289) or the beginning of the fourth century (A.D.301).

The streams of Christian influence – the 'Greek-type' from the north western borders and the 'Syrian-type' from the south western borders – penetrated into Armenia and at first continued to coexist side by side all through the fourth century. In addition paganism persisted long after the adherence of Armenia to Christianity. The centuries-old institutions and traditions of Zoroastrians and Mazdeism could not be eradicated altogether by a royal decree or by anti-pagan measures taken by the State.

The orientation of Armenia towards the west was irrevocable after the acceptance of Christianity, with all its cultural, social and political implications. To preserve the Christian tradition the ancient pagan conception of the world was imperceptibly transformed into one which was both Christian and western. And to keep it so, Armenia's powerful neighbours often intruded in the sphere of ecclesiastical life of the Armenian church and exerted pressure to bring about a solution of dogmatic disputes favourable to various political considerations.

In the wake of such developments, political and religious factors combined to counter-balance the increasing tide of Christian influence in the country. One faction favoured the revival of pagan religion in Armenia, whereas another faction became defenders of Christianity, though sometimes fearing its strength and trying to reduce it or bring it under control.

The early history of the Armenian church offers a bewildering picture of numerous movements, anti-ecclesiastical dissensions, and sects whose relations to each other can seldom be proved directly, but certain features of which frequently suggest points of contact. Their tendency either towards extreme asceticism, surpassing and distorting the ethical teaching of Christianity, or preaching greater moral rigorism than was compatible with the practice of the church. Sects like the Manichaean, Messalian, Encratite, Montanist and Novatianist, which flourished in Asia Minor between the first and the eighth centuries, found fertile ground in Armenia. This situation is attested by Movsēs Xorenac'i who, reflecting upon the period after the deaths of Sahak Part'ev and Mesrop Maštoc', comments in his *History* that 'the peace was disturbed, chaos became rooted, orthodoxy was shaken, and heterodoxy was established through ignorance'. Such a situation prepared the ground for and facilitated the spread of anti-ecclesiastical dissensions referred to by the historian with the customary invectives and perorations as 'brigands', 'schismatics', 'opponents of sound doctrine', 'dissentient tongues . . . who rise up in opposition to the wholesome teaching'.

The present study is a working synthesis of the state of research on religious movements in the Armenian church from the fourth to the tenth centuries. Religious movements have been an integral part of the Armenian church, and their growth is a phenomenon which runs side by side with, often directly influencing, such well-known developments as the rise of authority, the growth of canon law, and the nature of church-state relations.

The movements in the Armenian church played an important, if diversified, role in shaping Armenia's attitude towards Byzantium, Iranian interference in the country's religious life, the spread of Hellenism, and the Caliphate. With the end of the monarchy, the danger of annexation caused the Armenians to espouse ethnic, social and cultural separatism which expressed itself in religious terms.

Every historian of heresy must encounter the conflict of emphasis between the supporters of religious and of socio-economic factors as prime movers in the genesis of heresy. The first necessity is to examine the religious climate of orthodoxy in order to understand the deviations from it. On the other hand concrete information on the origins, social class and wealth of the sectarians will indicate the subtle social and economic background of these movements.

The history of Armenian sectarianism is a history of failure, for none of the movements surveyed succeeded either in imposing their views or in gaining tolerance for their opinions and practices in the Armenian church. Condemnation of their beliefs and practices as heretical, both by the church and the state led to effective extinction.

I am grateful to Professor D. M. Nicol for his guidance and help during the course of this research, and to Mr. E. V. Gulbekian for his comments on the typescript. This book is published with gratefully acknowledged financial assistance from the Armenian General Benevolent Union (European section), and His Eminence Abp. Torkom Manoogian, Primate of the Eastern Diocese of the Armenian Church in America.

CHAPTER I

SURVEY OF THE PRINCIPAL SOURCES

Knowledge of Armenian history for the period under consideration is derived from a variety of widely differing Armenian, Arabic, Byzantine and Syrian sources. The general course of events in its main outline is supplied by the Armenian sources which differ considerably in quality, detail and accuracy. The picture is then completed and sometimes corrected by information derived from the Arabic and Byzantine sources. This brief survey indicates the most important evidence.

Chronologically the first major source for the period is Sebēos's *Patmut'iwn Herakli* (History of Heraclius). The work covers the events between 590-661 and is a contemporary account. Sebēos relates the appearance of the Arabs as an event fulfilling divine prophecy in terms of the Book of Daniel, VII:3-24. The *History* by Sebēos was first published in Constantinople (1851) followed by St. Petersburg (1879) and Erevan (1939). The first Russian translation by K'. Patkanean published in St. Petersburg (1862) has been superseded by S. Malxasean's translation published in Erevan (1939). The *History* was translated into French by F. Macler (Paris 1904).

Patmut'iwn Łewondeay meci vardapeti Hayoc' (History of Łewond the Eminent, *vardapet* of the Armenians) is the next major source. It covers the history of a short period from A.D. 632-778. One original feature of Łewond's *History* is that while concentrating on the external political events he pays considerable attention to the internal situation in Armenia. The Armenian uprisings against the Caliphate in 703, 747-750 and 774-775 are described in great detail. Łewond's *History* incorporates the correspondence between the Umayyad caliph 'Umar II (717-720) and the Byzantine emperor Leo III the Isaurian (717-741), source material for the study of the history of iconoclasm. The English translation and discussion of the text is contained in A. Jeffery's "Ghevond's text of the correspondence between 'Umar and Leo III", *HTR* 37 (1944), 269-332.

Contrary to the view expressed by A. Jeffery and J. Meyendorff ("Byzantine view of Islam", *DOP* 18 (1964)), S. Gero in his own research (*Byzantine iconoclasm during the reign of Leo III with particular attention to the oriental sources* (CSCO, Louvain 1973)) is convinced that the text of Łewond's correspondence is not original.

Łewond's *History* was first published in French translation by G. Šahnazarean (Paris, 1856) followed by the Armenian text (St. Petersburg, 1887). Two Russian translations are available, the first by K'. Patkanean (St. Petersburg, 1862) and the second by S. Malxasean with the critical Armenian text (St. Petersburg, 1887). The Revd. Zaven Arzoumanian's lucid translation of the *History of Łewond*, "the Eminent Vardapet of the Armenians" (Philadelphia, 1982), enriched by historical and textual notes fills a serious lacuna.

Yovhannēs Drasxanakertc'i (845-929) was kat'ołikos of all Armenians from 897-925/30 and took active part in the events described in the latter part of his important history. After the revolt of 850-852 against the Arabs, in 862 Ašot Bagratuni was given the title of "prince of princes" and by 885 the Armenian monarchy was restored.

To win the support of the Arabs, Yovhannēs Drasxanakertc'i travelled to Damascus to persuade the Arabs not to annex the territories of king Smbat I. Having failed in his mission he appealed to the Byzantine patriarch Nicholas Mysticus, as discussed by R. J. H. Jenkins in "Letter 101 of the patriarch Nicholas Mysticus" (*B*, XXI (1961) 75-80).

Two works have survived from his pen. The first *Šaric' hayrapetac'n Hayoc' yaytararut'iwn eranelwoyn Yovhannu kat'ołikosi*, which is a list of the names of Armenian kat'ołikoses from Saint Grigor the Illuminator to his own times, contained in *Hawak'munk' i groc' patmagrac'* (Collection from Historical Writings) by Samuēl Anec'i (Vałaršapat, 1893). The second is his *Patmut'iwn Hayoc'* (History of the Armenians) from the earliest period down to the year 924. The first half of the book relies heavily on the histories of the preceding centuries from Koriwn to Łewond. The latter half of the book contains an eye-witness account of all the events described. The oldest surviving manuscript of the *History* dates back to 1689 (Matenadaran no.1895). The Armenian text was published in Moscow (1853), Jerusalem (1867) and Tiflis (1912). A French translation by M. J. Saint-Martin appeared in Paris (1841).

T'ovma Arcruni, the royal historian, compiled his *Patmut'iwn tann Arcruneac'* (History of the Arcruni House) at the request of Grigor Derenik, ruler of Vaspurakan (died 885). For the early period of his history of the Arcrunis, T'ovma has consulted the works of Movsēs Xorenac'i, Koriwn, Mambrē *vercanoł* and from non-Armenian sources he has references to Eusebius of Caesarea, Philo of Alexandria and Herodotus. The *History* was first published in Constantinople (1852) from a manuscript dated A.D. 1303. The later two editions of St. Petersburg (1887) and Tiflis (1917) are reprints of the first publication. The French translation by M. Brosset is contained in *CHA*, I (1874), pp 4-263.

Movsēs Dasxuranc'i's *Patmut'iwn Ałwanic' ašxarhi* (The history of the land of the [Caucasian] Albanians) is the next important source for the study of the period. The earliest mention of the work occurs in Anania Mokac'i (943-967), followed by Uxt'anēs, and Step'annos Ōrbelean. In the works of the authors mentioned no name is attached to the history. The first author to mention the writer of the history is Mxit'ar

Goš (13th century). The *History* consists of three books. The first books contain extracts from the works of P'awstos, Ełišē, Xorenac'i, Agat'angełos and the *Girk' t'łt'oc'*. It is the second book, concerned with the events to which the author is contemporary, which is of great importance, not only for Armenian history but also for that of neighbouring countries.

The Armenian text of the *History*, with notes by K. Šahnazarean, was published in Paris (1860), also with notes by M. Ēmin in Moscow (1860) and reprinted in Tiflis (1912). The Russian translation by K'. Patkanean, published in St. Petersburg (1861), is incomplete. The modern Armenian translation by V. Afak'elyan appeared in Erevan (1969). The English translation of the *History* by C. J. F. Dowsett appeared in London (1961).

Step'anos Tarōnec'i Asołik is the best representative of 10th century Armenian historiography. From the province of Tarōn, he is better known in Armenian literature as Asołik (reciter), a surname which may be attributed to his skills in the art of music or oratory. His major work *Patmut'iwn tiezerakan* (Universal History) is an account of events down to A.D. 1004, written in the capital city of Ani at the request of Sargis kat'ołikos Sevanc'i. The history consists of three books; at the start of his work he provides a survey of the sources available to him.

Asołik's *History* was first published in Paris (1859), in a form which, due to lack of manuscripts, is inadequate. The second and best edition appeared in St. Petersburg (1885); this is a critical text of the history based on nine different manuscripts, with a useful introduction and notes by S. Malxasean. Also available are French translations by E. Dulaurier (Paris, 1883) and F. Macler (Paris, 1917), a Russian translation by H. Ēmin (Moscow, 1864), and a German translation by H. Gelzer and A. Burckhardt (Leipzig, 1907).

Aristakēs Lastiverc'i's *Patmut'iwn Hayoc'* (History of the Armenians) reflects on the events leading to the fall of the Bagratuni kingdom covering the period between 1000-1087. It gives a full account of the annexations of Armenian territories by Byzantium, beginning with Karin (949), then Tarōn (966/67), Tayk (1000), Vaspurakan (1021/22), and Ani (1045). In 1047-48 began the Seljuq invasions and the eventual fall of the kingdom in 1064. Aristakēs has devoted chapters 22 and 23 of his history to the manifestation of the heresy of the T'ondrakec'is, the English translation of which can be found in *The Key of Truth* (Oxford, 1898).

The first publication by the Mxit'arean fathers of Venice (1844) was reprinted in Venice (1901) and Tiflis (1921). The critical edition with notes and introduction by K. Yuzbašyan appeared in Erevan (1968) followed by the Russian translation in 1971. The French translation by M. Canard and H. Berberian was published in the series *Editions de Byzantion*, 5 (Bruxelles, 1973).

The majority of the historical writings surviving in Arabic date from the 'Abbasid period. The leading historian of the Arab conquests of the Caucasus is the Persian, Aḥmad ibn-Yaḥya al-Balādhurī (died 892). His main work *Futūḥ al-Buldān* integrates the many stories of the conquests of the various cities and lands into one comprehensive whole. In this book a separate chapter is devoted to *The conquest of Armenia.*

Abu Dj'afar Muḥammad ibn Djarīr al-Ṭabarī (839-923) who was born in Tabaristan, whence the name Ṭabarī, is the author of a remarkable and accurate history *Ta'rīkh al-Rusul wa'l-Mulūk* (Annals of the Apostles and kings). The history begins with the creation of the world and goes down to A.D. 915. The events are arranged chronologically under the successive years of the Hidjrah. Ibn-al Athīr (1160-1234) abridged in his *Kamil fī'l Ta'rīkh* (General History) al-Ṭabarī's *Annals* with occasional additions from other sources extending the narrative to A.D. 1231. Abū-'l-Ḥasan 'Alī al-Mas'ūdī (died 956) styled the "Herodotus of the Arabs" is the author of an encyclopaedic historico-geographical work *Murūdj al-Dhahab wa-Ma'-ādin al-Djawhar* (Meadows of gold and mines of gems). It is a universal history of events grouped around dynasties, kings and peoples beginning with the creation down to A.D. 947.

The first geographical treatise in Arabic to give detailed information on the administration, the socio-political situation, the taxation system, roads and cities of the caliphate is Ibn Khurradādhbih (died c.912), author of *Kitāb al-Masālik wa'l-Mamālik* (Book of the roads and countries), the oldest geographical work in Arabic that has come down to us.

In 891-92 al-Ya'ḳūbī, who worked in Armenia and Khurāsān, produced his *Kitāb al-Buldān* (Book of countries) which describes the principal towns of the caliphate and gives an account of the economic conditions of everyday life in the occupied countries.

Many of these works have been translated into modern European languages. The Armenian translations of the sections relevant to Armenian history are found in al-Balādhurī, *HA*, 1, 2, 4, 6, 8 (1903); al-Ya'ḳūbī, *Bazmavēp*, 9-10, 11-12 (1957) and 3-5 (1958); Ibn al-Athīr, *HA*, 2, 4 (1908) and 3 (1909) and al-Ṭabarī, *HA*, 5, 8 (1905) and 9 (1906).

Among the Byzantine sources the most important is Constantine Porphyrogenitus's *De Administrando Imperio*, edited by G. Moravcsik (Budapest, 1949); commentary by F. Dvornik and R. J. H. Jenkins (University of London, 1962). Chapters 43-46 concern Armenia. Written on the basis of Byzantine diplomatic documents, they contain a detailed account of the imperial relations with the princes of Tarōn from the beginning of the 10th century up to and including the reign of Romanus I (920-944). Chapter 44 is devoted to establishing the Byzantine claim to the territory of Apahunik' and with the history of the Ḳaysite emirs of Manazkert. Chapter 45 is a diplomatic history with instruction on policy to be followed with regard to the lands near Theodosiopolis. Chapter 46 is an account of the failure of a diplomatic manœuvre by Romanus I to annex Ardanouǰ. The Armenian translation of Chapters 43-46, with introduction and notes can be found in H. Bart'ikyan, *Byuzandakan ałbyurner. II. Kostandin Ciranacin* (Erevan, 1970). The Byzantine sources on the Paulicians include *A History of the Paulicians* by Peter of Sicily, *A History of the Manichaeans* attributed to Photius, a *Treatise* attributed to Peter the Higumen, and *Abjuration Formulae*

(Greek texts with French translation see *Travaux et Mémoires*, 4, (1970)).

Many of the Armenian sources regarding the sects are ambiguous in that they do not relate to any specific sect, but are nevertheless indispensable for the study of the early religious developments in Armenia.

The philosophical and theological treatise of Eznik Kołbac'i called *Ełc ałandoc'* (The refutation of sects), written between 443-448, is an attempt to vindicate the truth of the Christian faith against heretical factions within the church. This work, preserved in a single manuscript dated 1280, was first printed in Smyrna (1762) and then in Constantinople (1763) and Venice (1826, 1850, 1863, 1914, 1926). The great scholars of Eznik, L. Mariès and C. Mercier published an annotated edition of the work with French translation in *Patrologia Orientalis*, XXVIII (1959). A German translation was made by J. M. Schmidt, *Wider die Sekten* (Vienna, 1900). A modern Armenian version, with introduction and commentary by A. A. Abrahamyan, appeared in Erevan (1970).

References to the Borborites and Messalians can be found in the works of Armenian hagiographers and historians of the fifth century. Of particular interest is Koriwn's *Vark' Maštoc'i* (The life of Maštoc') edited by M. Abełyan (Erevan, 1941 and 1962) and Movsēs Xorenac'i's *Patmut'iwn Hayoc'* (History of the Armenians, Tiflis, 1913). From the early period mention ought to be made of the *Girk' tłt'oc'* (Book of Letters) a collection of documents, official letters and treatises on the history of the Armenian church, being chiefly the correspondence between various Armenian, Georgian, Syrian and Byzantine personages. It is composed of three groups of documents dating respectively from the fifth to the seventh century, from the eighth to the eleventh century, and from the eleventh to the thirteenth century. The letters of the patriarch of Constantinople, Atticus (405-425), to Saint Sahak, of Grigor Magistros to the Syrian Patriarch, of Nersēs Šnorhali and Paul of Tarōn, and the *Oath of Union* are a few of the documents relevant to our study. Partial translations from the *Book of Letters* (Tiflis, 1901) can be found in M. Tallon, *Livre des Lettres* (Beyrouth, 1955); N. Garsoïan, *The Paulician heresy* (The Hague, 1967); F. C. Conybeare, ed., *The Key of Truth* (Oxford, 1898) and L. Frivold, *The Incarnation. A study of the doctrine of the Incarnation in the Armenian Church in the 5th and 6th centuries according to the Book of Letters* (Universitetsforlaget, 1981). To this group of early sources belongs also the *Kanonagirk' Hayoc'* (Book of Armenian canons). Some parts of these were published by A. Łlčean in Tiflis (1913). A more up-to-date critical edition prepared by V. Hakobyan appeared in Erevan in two volumes in 1964 and 1971.

CHAPTER II

A HISTORY OF THE RELIGIOUS SECTS IN ARMENIA: FOURTH TO TENTH CENTURIES

Christianity having liberated itself from its Jewish past, following the destruction of Jerusalem in A.D. 70, found itself in conflict with the beliefs and ideas of the surrounding Hellenism. The new conflict threatened to distort the faith from within, and the second century was marked by intense struggle as Christians strove to preserve the purity and integrity of their doctrine. The church had first to protect itself from all attempts to reconcile Christianity too easily with the spirit of Hellenism. If the church had remained in the Jewish mould it would not have conquered the gentile world and if it had simply adapted Hellenistic thought it would not have survived in the form we know today.

Gnosticism, a generic term used primarily to refer to theosophical adaptations of Christianity propagated by a dozen or more rival sects which rose within the early church between A.D. 80 and 150, became Christianity's most redoubtable opponent. The adherents of the Gnostic movement laid claim to a secret knowledge or gnosis which transcended the simple faith of the Church. With its emphasis on this hidden knowledge, drawing various strands of view of the world from neo-Platonism, Hellenized Zoroastrianism, and Judaism blended into a systematic doctrine, Gnosticism offered a sort of cosmological scheme according to which the spiritual elements in the world were gradually freed from the captivity of matter. The Gnostics regarded the material world as utterly alien to the supreme God and to goodness, and therefore as the creation of inferior powers. The natural order of things reflected nothing at all of the divine glory and heavenly beauty. The world was in the iron control of evil powers and therefore much time was devoted to an ascetic life with rules for the mortification of the flesh and the special prohibition on marriage.

The Gnostic devaluation of the created order led some sects which stood closest to Christianity, such as the groups founded by Basilides and Valentinus, to reject any incarnation. It was inconceivable to them that the divine Christ could have come "in the flesh" in any ultimately true sense. Although Christ was acknowledged as the Logos, Saviour and Redeemer, the essence of Christianity as faith in the Incarnation of

God and His coming into the world was rejected. The Church combated the many forms and systems of this great movement in the compendious catalogues and refutations of heresy that issued from the pens of the Christian fathers from the second to the fifth centuries. All subsequent movements in the early Church to a certain degree adopted and developed or fought against a particular concept of Gnosticism.

Gnosticism had its share of influence also on the progress and development of Armenian Christianity. Sectarian movements have played an important role in the history of Armenia. From the very beginning the church had to combat a number of sects, among them the Borborites and the *Mcłnēs*, the Paulicians and the T'ondrakec'is. A sect referred to in the Armenian sources under the names *borboriton, barbarianos, barbarismos, borbiosk, borboriosk'* entered Armenia from Syria. The name of the original sect remains obscure, for Armenian writers have wrongly transcribed or interpreted the name as originating from the Greek term *borboros* which means "filth, mud". The Armenian compendious catalogue and refutations of heresy *Girk' herjuacoc'* (The book of heresies) lists a number of sects of which the 130th is named as the sect of the *borboriosk'*, called the "muddy ones", who commit all evils without exception. In Armenian dictionaries the term means simply "filth".

Our first sources of information on the sect are the historian Movsēs Xorenac'i and Koriwn *vardapet*, the contemporary and biographer of Mesrop Maštoc'. In his *History*, Xorenac'i cites a letter from the patriarch of Constantinople, Atticus (405-25), to St. Sahak in which the former grants permission to St. Sahak to preach in western Armenia on condition that he will attempt "either to convert the sect of the Borborites or to expel them from your see".[1]

Koriwn in his account of Maštoc''s teaching activities incidentally refers also to his work among the sectarians. "Then he undertook to examine the uncouth and stubborn sect of the Borborites (*Barbarianos*). And when he found no other way to rectify them, he began to use the misery inflicting stick, with very severe chastisements, imprisonments, tortures. And when even then they remained unrepentant and deprived of salvation, they were scourged, branded, smeared in soot, subjected to various indignities, and driven out of the land."[2] In relation to the preaching of the Gospel in the remote regions of Armenia, in the province of Gołt'n, Koriwn says "taking along with him his faithful pupils, the blessed one [Maštoc'] went to the disorderly and uncultivated region of Gołt'n. He was met by the ruler of Gołt'n, a pious man whose name was Šabit' . . . , and the blessed one at once exercising the art of preaching, with the faithful co-operation of the ruler began [to preach] in the region, and capture them all away from their native traditions of satanic idolatry and turned them to obedience to Christ."[3]

According to Movsēs Xorenac'i, when Maštoc' returned to Armenia, the kat'ołikos Sahak authorised him to preach in western Armenia instructing him to "examine the pestilential Borborites, and if they would not come to orthodoxy by persuasion without force, to persecute them with tortures, that they might exact vengeance like enemies from enemies and by a just death the unjust death of souls might be put to shame."[4]

It has been suggested that the Borborites are the Messalians under a more abusive name, but Epiphanius treats the Borborites as a definite movement of Gnostic origin. Melk'onyan suggested that we should see at the root of the name the Syriac word *Barbarit* meaning "sons of the desert".[5] Conybeare identified the Borborites with the Nestorians. This view has been dismissed on the grounds that the missionary work of Maštoc' took place between the years A.D. 415-423, while Nestorianism was condemned as a heresy at the council of Ephesus in A.D. 431. Besides, it is difficult to accept the implied suggestion that the patriarch of Constantinople entrusted the investigation and persecution of Nestorianism to an Armenian *vardapet*. Others have identified the Borborites with another Armenian sect called the *Mcłnē*.

The term *Mcłnē* derives from the Aramaic *ṣla* which means to pray and the derivative adjective *mṣalin* meaning "one who prays". The name of the sect *mêṣallêyānē* has given rise to the Greek term Messalians. Messalians, also known as the Euchites, were a pietistic mendicant sect. They appear to have originated in Mesopotamia around A.D. 300 and thence to have spread to Syria, Armenia, Asia Minor and Thrace. The radical form of ascetism which they preached maintained that the key to the problem of human salvation was a complete break with the world: a denial of literally every form of labour or activity that belonged to the world.

Parallel to this they also held the view that in each man there is an indwelling devil who can be ejected, not by sacramental grace but exclusively by intense prayer and ascetic contemplation sufficient to produce palpable inward feelings. They abandoned the world and all their possessions in order to give themselves entirely to the life of prayer, and this to such a complete extent that they would have nothing to do even with the pious practice of fasting. For the same reason they did not work, they had no homes of their own, but gathered by begging what they needed to live on. This means that they did not resort to the desert, but remained in contact with the rest of the community. This movement has particular importance in Armenian history.

In A.D. 447, a council of the Armenian church was called at Šahapivan for the purpose of removing all the pagan survivals still persisting in the life of the people. It was a council which dealt predominantly with moral questions, with the reformation of the church, which had not yet been rid of the ancient pagan customs and traditions. Some of the canons of the council are specifically concerned with the *Mcłnē* sect. "Let no bishop or priest or deacon or any member of the clergy or of a congregation keep any kind of housekeeper as is the custom of the *Mcłnē*. If anyone should have one, and this be confirmed by the testimony of witnesses, let him be deposed from his order, whatever it be, and let him be considered impious and a layman."

"If any one be found in *Mcłnēut'iwn*, whether he be a priest or a deacon or a monk, let him be deprived of his priestly orders, let him be branded on the face with the sign of a fox, and let him be confined for penance to a place of hermitage. Then if he be found again, let him be hamstrung on both legs and be sent to a leper refuge, for the man was held in honour and did not know. Let the same punishment be visited on a monk. Further, if men be found in the sect with their wives and children, let the women, and children who have reached the age of reason be hamstrung, branded on the face with the sign of a fox and sent for penance to a leper refuge; as for the children who have not reached the age of reason and do not know the pollution, let them be taken away and given into the hands of the holy servants of the church to be brought up and educated in the true faith and the fear of God."

"If there be found any evildoer among the people and the priest has learned of this and not reported it to the bishop; if this be found true upon investigation and the priest has known the matter for many days and months before and not addressed a complaint to the bishop, let the canonical punishment for *Mcłnē* be borne also by the priests and let them not perform their priestly office for the rest of their lives . . . Then if the priests have reported to the bishop, and this be supported by the testimony of witnesses, and the bishop either accept a bribe and cover it up or show partiality, and if this be shown by the testimony of witnesses, namely that the complaint of the priests really reached his ear and he disdained God's command and did not go out to seek him who was lost, and was not jealous and an avenger of God's law, let him be deposed from his see who hid the adulterer, and let the priest be acknowledged innocent. But if the bishop was diligent and an avenger, and the priests and other men bear witness to the bishop's labours, and he report about the evildoer to the authorities, but the prince of the country, or the chief *naxarar* of any village, or the lord of a province, wishes to be the protector of uncleanliness and to hide the adulterer, either for the silver of perdition or from partiality or favour, and does not prefer to love Christ and his commands and to be an avenger of the laws of the Lord and of the spirit and the flesh, let such a one be accursed and let him be cut off from the holy Church until he shall deliver the polluted one into the hands of the bishop. And if the pollution be found in the house of the *naxarar*, either in his wife, or his daughter, or his son, or in himself, and he should not hand his family over to the bishop and himself return to holiness, but should wish to be their tyrannical refuge, let him be accursed with all his house, his kin and his life. Let him not dare come out into a public place, let not his friends and all the world consort with him until he shall have gone from his uncleanliness and come to the holy Church. And if he be not in the uncleanliness [himself] let him hand over his household and his servants into the hands of the chief bishop for rebuke . . . And if he [the *ostikan*], himself, with his household, be found in *mcłnēut'iwn*, let him be seized together with his polluted household and let him be brought for judgement before the chief bishop and before the great princes and the leading judges, and let them jointly avenge the laws of God so that others, beholding this, in holiness and fear, should revere the Creator of all."[6]

Towards the end of the fifth century, the historian Łazar P'arpec'i, was accused of heretical tendencies. To vindicate himself he wrote a letter to his sponsor Vahan Mamikonean. The letter is not as explicit as we might wish, for it declines to name the heresy because it was, as he says, such an abominable one that he did not deem it decent to write about it. The identification is made even more difficult when we are told by Łazar that "concerning the *heresy of the Armenians* of which they speak, it is anonymous as regards its teacher, and unwritten as regards its teaching". After a little vague abuse he then declares that one can apply to them the proverb "for the bride of the swine, a bath of drain water" (II Peter 2:22). This *Armenian heresy* has been identified with the Messalians.

In the canons of the council of Šahapivan there is nothing on the main tenets of the Messalians. The characteristic tenets of the sect on perpetual prayer, the doctrine of the two souls, the presence of Satan in the human soul, the state of imperturbability attained through constant prayer – whence the sect's other name, the Enthusiasts – are never mentioned. It is hard to understand how the Church fathers could have overlooked these heretical concepts had they been present among the sect in question, especially since the Messalians had already been condemned by the council of Sidē in A.D. 390 and by bishop Flavian of Antioch (381 - 404). St. Melik'-Bašxyan has also rightly observed that the one *Mcłnē* tenet condemned in the canons of Šahapivan, the maintenance of a "housekeeper" by members of the clergy cannot be reconciled with what we know of Messalian asceticism, repudiation of all property and labour. We are driven to the conclusion that the *Mcłnē* heresy had nothing in common with the Messalians.[7]

In the Armenian *Book of Canons* the *Mcłnē* are alluded to in canon thirty-two, ascribed to kat'ołikos Yovhannēs Ōjnec'i: "It is not fitting for any one to be found in the places of that most wicked *Mcłnē* sect who are called Polikeank', nor to adhere to them, nor speak to them, nor visit them, but one should retreat from them altogether, to execrate them and pursue them with hatred, for they are the sons of Satan, fuel for the eternal fires, and alienated from the love of the Creator's will."[8]

Subsequently the historian Aristakēs Lastiverc'i characterises the T'ondrakec'i sect: ". . . their *mcłnē* [filthy] observances we deem it indecent to commit to writing."[9] Also particularly interesting is the use of the word in a manuscript in the form "concerning the evil heresy of the *mcłnē* who are *paylikeank'*."[10] The word *payl* has the same meaning as the word *mcłnē*, namely "filth" and so the translation of both the terms used in this form means those who are "filthy in life". This is the form of the name used by kat'ołikos Yovhannēs Ōjnec'i in his treatise against the Paulicians: "*naxkin mcłnēut'ean payłakenut'ean* (the first incestuous and filthy remnants of the Paulicians) who had endured a thorough rebuke from Nersēs the kat'ołikos, but by no means mindful of it, they fled after his death and hid somewhere in our land." This is the first direct allusion to the Paulicians, which was the next major movement in the Armenian church to concern the church authorities.

First of all it must be emphasised that these sectarians were called Paulicians by their opponents and that this was not a name they gave to themselves. "The Paulicians" – says Peter the monk – "call themselves Christians and they call us Romans."[11] The same point is affirmed by Peter of Sicily[12] and the Armenian author Grigor Magistros.[13] It is natural to suppose that in the name which they gave themselves they expressed the conviction that it was they, the sectarians, who were the bearers and preservers of the true Christian teaching, while the "Romans" had strayed from the truth. The feeling for primitive Christianity is remarkable both in the ideology and in the practices of the Paulicians.[14] In insisting that they were "Christians" the heretics rejected the name *Paulician* equally deliberately because it was attributed to them by their enemies. But it is under this name that they were widely known both in the east and, subsequently, in the west.

In Greek texts this name is found in the form παυλικιανός. In the Armenian documents we find the most diverse forms and spellings: *Pawłikean-k'*[15], *Paylikean-k'*[16], *Pōlikean-k'd*[17], *Pawlikean-k'*[18], *Pōlikean-k'*[19], *Pōłikeank'*[20], *Pollikean-k'*[21].

Examining the spelling in the canons of the council of Dvin, K. Ter Mkrttschian puts forward the objection that neither *Pōllikean* nor *Paylakenut'iwn* can be derived from the Greek παυλικιανός. His argument is based on the fact that in the Armenian form, against all expectations, there are two "l"s and an "o" (in place of "ō" = aw, corresponding to the Greek "*αυ*"). The name itself comes from the name Paul, and in conformity with the rules of the Armenian language, it is not difficult to see in this word the diminutive syllable "ik" and the suffix of belonging "ean". Thus Ter Mkrttschian concludes that the form of the name Paulician is not Greek but Armenian in origin.[22]

It is a fact that oriental names are mostly deformed in Greek, while the form παυλικιανός corresponds too closely to its supposed original. It is thus reasonable to suppose that we are dealing with a Greek formation of a name, based on the Greek form of the Armenian name Pawłik. Names ending in "ik" are hellenised by the addition of the suffix "ios" whether the "ik" is a root as in Gagik Κακίκιος or a suffix as in Grigorik Κρικόρικιος. In the present case we are quite justified in expecting a form like παυλίκιος from which comes quite regularly παυλικιανός. This way of forming the Greek names of heretics, parallel to the Armenian seems the most reasonable.

E. Tēr Minasyan, analysing the form of the name occurring in the *Oath of Union*, says that it is simply a result of misunderstanding. The link between the term *Pawłikean* and the name *Pawłik* was no longer perceived; the feeling that it was an adjective was also lost and this led to the declension of the name on another model, i.e. *keank'*, *kenac'*.[23] From the form *Paylikean* the substantive *Payłakenut'iwn* was formed, which is attested only in one place, *Against the Paulicians* by Yovhannēs Ōjnec'i.[24] Ačaṙyan supposed that this word, which is the parallel of *Payłakumn* (blindness), was applied to the heretics because it sounded like their own name.[25] But Abełyan, recognising that the form *Payłakenut'iwn* resulted from the root *Payłak* as in *Payłakumn*, also meaning "blindness" or "blindly", considered that kat'ołikos Yovhannēs Ōjnec'i was using the word to characterise the Armenian Messalians.[26]

Bartikyan suggests that by *Payłakenut'iwn* Yovhannēs Ōjnec'i probably means the heresy of Paul of Samosata, bishop of Antioch, frequently confused both in the middle ages and nowadays with the heresy of the Paulicians, on account of a similarity of names but otherwise completely different heresies.[27] It is difficult to understand what confusion Bart'ikyan is referring to, for the word *Payłakenut'iwn* refers back to the contemporaries of Yovhannēs Ōjnec'i, the Armenian Paulicians, and the form of the name is apparently suggested by one of the dialectal forms of the name *Payłikeank'* examined above.

The Arab sources preserve the name of the heretics in forms like *Baylakānī, al Bayālika*[28], which goes back to the Armenian form of the name *Paylik-ean-k'*. The Latin sources have kept the Greek forms of the name *Paulikiani, Pauliciáni*, and also a different interpretation *Publicani, Populicani, Poblicani, Poplicani.*[29] These names were affixed, by the western Christian ecclesiastical authorities, to people convicted of heresy in Oxford in 1160, in Flanders in 1162, and in Burgundy in 1167. At the third Lateran council held in 1179, the Publicani were condemned and were identified with the Albigenses, Cathari and Patarini.

To which Paul do the Paulicians owe their names? It has been suggested that the Paulicians were so called after the Apostle Paul, for according to the sources, the Paulicians revered Paul, their leaders took the names of Paul's disciples and the Paulician communities and churches were claimed to be founded by Paul. Addressing himself to his followers in Kibossa (Macedonia) Constantine declares "You are Macedonians, I am Silvanus sent to you by Paul."[30] His successors in the leadership of the Paulicians followed his example by each taking the name of someone who was associated with St. Paul in the Acts of the Apostles or in St. Paul's Epistles, and by naming each new Paulician church that they founded after one of those founded by St. Paul.[31] Pauline concepts and manners of thinking are found in various Paulician doctrines.

Paul the Apostle who is the pillar of orthodoxy could not have been considered as the founder of a sect by the Christians who were so opposed to the Paulicians. The Paulicians on the other hand, by affiliating themselves with the Apostle, derived certain authority and prestige, although, the heretics rejected the name Paulician and their own name for themselves was "True Believers".

In the Greek sources, positive information has been preserved on the origin of the name of the movement. In the *Treatise* of Peter the Monk, which is certainly older than the *History* of Peter of Sicily and was apparently used by the latter, it is said "The Paulicians, themselves Manichaeans, were called, unlike the Manichaeans, after a certain Paul of Samosata, son of a Manichaean woman Kallinike, who had two sons, the same Paul and John. Kallinike sent them from Samosata to the theme of Armeniakon, there to spread the Manichaean heresy. The village where they arrived was re-named Episparis (seedbed) and the disciples of Kallinike's sons were Paulicians."[32] In Peter of Sicily we find a similar account of the events. He tells how some of Mani's disciples came to Samosata from Armenia[33], and turned the inhabitants of the country from their right path, and how their false doctrines began to spread rapidly. Kallinike, an inhabitant of Samosata, sent her son Paul to the village of Phanaroia where he began to preach their heresy. From this time, continues the author, the village changed its name and was called Episparis. As for the heresy, it began to be called by the name of its preacher, for from that moment the renegades among the Manichaeans took another name – that of the Paulicians.[34]

Patriarch Photius's *History*, which is largely based on the *Treatise* of Peter the Monk and the *History* of Peter of Sicily, also speaks of Kallinike and her sons. As with the other two authors, Kallinike lived not in Armenian Samosata, but the Samosata in

Syria. Paul and John appear in the theme of Armeniakon and first of all in Phanaroia. One of the villages received the name Episparis. The renegades, continues Photius, having renounced the name Christian, began to call themselves Paulicians after one of Kallinike's sons. "Others, however, say that the name Paulician comes not from one of the sons of Kallinike but from the combination of both, from which resulted a barbarous name Pauloioannai and then instead of the Pauloioannai they began to be called Paulicians (Παυλικιανοί).[35]

Peter of Sicily and Photius, who seem to agree on the authenticity of the above account, return to this theme in describing the cruel measures taken against the Paulicians during the first half of the reign of Justinian II, that is not later than 695, when the arrested heretics were burned. "One of them called Paul, an Armenian by birth and having two sons, Genesius and Theodore, escaped and appeared at Episparis, about which we have spoken in detail above when writing about Paul and John of Samosata, sons of Kallinike. It is from this Paul that the heretics took the name of Paulicians in order to distinguish themselves from the Manichaeans. Paul sent his son Genesius to do his impious preaching and gave him the name Timothy."[36] Photius recounts this incident in similar fashion but concerning the change of name he remarks: "a large number of the partisans of impiety think that the filthy Manichaeans received their name rather from this Paul the Armenian than from the son of Kallinike."[37] This is the limit of the positive information the sources offer on the origin of the name Paulician, which goes back either to Paul of Samosata, son of Kallinike, or Paul and his brother John, or finally Paul the Armenian, father of Genesius and Theodore.

Conybeare has supposed that the name derives from Paul of Samosata, bishop of Antioch, who was accused of turning away from the official Christology of the Christian Church. According to him the name "Pauliciani is simply the Armenian form of Pauliani"[38], and is a reference not to St. Paul, but to the last great champion of Adoptionist Christianity in the Greek world, Paul of Samosata. The information of the Greek sources on the origin of the name as coming from the son of Kallinike, has in view the bishop of Antioch. It is quite possible that the name of the latter's mother was Kallinike.

Bart'ikyan also arrives at a similar conclusion: "In all probability this legend was created later by the Orthodox clergy. It is not difficult to see in the person of Paul of Samosata, son of the Manichaean woman Kallinike, the celebrated heretical leader Paul of Samosata, the patriarch of Antioch." We do not doubt, continues Bart'ikyan, "that what contributed to the creation of this legend was first the names of the heretics linked with Paul and secondly the fact that the first leader of the Paulicians, Constantine-Sylvanus, appeared in the town of Samosata, that is Armenian Samosata, which was the cradle of Paulician heresy."

The tendency of the church to present Paulicianism as the resurrection or second growth of the Manichaean heresy also contributed to the creation of the figure of the Manichaean woman Kallinike, mother of Paul; but "the Paulianists have no connection with the Paulicians."[39] Bart'ikyan then demonstrated how the Greek writers muddled the names. In the manuscript variants of the canons of the council of Nicaea, the name

Παυλιανισταί is replaced by Παυλικιανοί. Following this, Zonaras substitutes Paulianists for Paulicians.[40] Theodore Balsamon, patriarch of Antioch, supposes that the Paulianists are the Paulicians named after Paul son of Kallinike.[41]

Similar examples of identifications of Paulicians-Paulianists are given by Garsoian, who, unlike Bart'ikyan, insists that there is a certain similarity of doctrine between the teachings of Paul of Samosata and the Paulicians.[42] Conybeare and Garsoian, suggest this identification on the basis of the supposition that *The Key of Truth*, the work of the Armenian Ōhannēs which was discovered in the 80s of the eighteenth century, is an authentic work and an organic part of Paulicianism.[43]

In addition to the arguments brought forward by Bart'ikyan, Garsoian turns her attention towards other evidence which, in her opinion, confirms beyond doubt the theory that Paulicianism derives from Paul of Samosata.[44] She quotes the specific identifications of the Paulicians with Paul of Samosata made by both the Armenian and the Byzantine writers. Grigor Magistros describes the T'ondrakec'is in the following manner: "Here then you see the Paulicians who got their poison from Paul of Samosata."[45] Peter of Sicily points out that the Paulicians of Tephrikē hypocritically anathematized Mani and other heretics and Paul of Samosata as well.[46] According to Garsoian the evidence of the Byzantine sources on Paul of Samosata, son of Kallinike, must be interpreted in the same way. The identification of Mas'ūdī is unquestionable, ". . . al-bayālika . . . these follow the heresy of Paul of Samosata, one of the first Patriarchs of Antioch."[47]

Much of the above evidence is susceptible to another interpretation. Grigor Magistros was familiar with the Greek sources on the Paulicians. In identifying the T'ondrakec'is with the Paulicians and in complete agreement with the Greek tradition, he accuses them of Manichaeanism. Could not the allusion to Paul of Samosata be a reference to Paul, son of Kallinike? The remark of Peter of Sicily that "the Paulicians throw anathema on Mani and his filthy followers, as they do on Paul of Samosata"[48], is further strengthened by a similar statement by Peter the Monk that "the Paulicians curse both Mani, Paul and John."[49]

A number of sources point to the conclusion that several of the authors of the middle ages who identified the Paulicians with the Paulianists were inadequately informed. Their conception that Paulicianism comes from Paulianism is a conjecture based entirely on the resemblance of names of Kallinike's son and the bishop of Antioch. This view is unfounded and the result of a confusion "which cannot be justified either doctrinally or historically, (and must) be finally abandoned."[50]

In a special article devoted to the study of the origin of the name, Loos comes to the conclusion that Paul, son of Kallinike, is a historical person who played an essential role in the life and history of the Paulician sect. Later tradition identified him with the celebrated heretic Paul of Samosata, the third-century bishop of Antioch. That this was so is evident from the formula of Abjuration and the legend about the Manichaean woman named Kallinike.[51]

The historicity of Paul, son of Kallinike, is confirmed by the Abjuration formula of the Paulicians. Article six proclaims: "Anathema on those who reject or deform the four Gospels of our Lord and the epistles of the apostle Paul and in place of God, creator of all the existing world, worship the so-called ruler of this world, and instead of the holy apostle Paul honour Paul, son of Kallinike, and four of his disciples, received as the four gospels, and call the three others the Holy Trinity."[52] In Article nine are anathematized those who reject the apostles and their teaching but accept and revere six Paulician disciples who deformed evangelical doctrines and the gospels themselves, that is Paul, Silvanus, Titus, Timothy, Epaphroditus and Tychicus.[53] These formulae grossly distort Paulician doctrine; for example, they call on the heretics to recognise the holiness of the apostle Paul, who was already venerated by them to an extreme degree. However, the fact that they mention Paul, son of Kallinike, in the list of undoubtedly historical leaders of the sect, speaks in favour of the historicity of the latter.

In the Armenian legend, included in the Armenian version of John of Damascus's *Heresies* in Chapter 154, the following story appears:

> Behold a certain woman named Šetʻi, this woman having come after the Arabs, came to the Armenians. And a certain Pōł from the province of Ayrarat, who was a disciple of St. Ephrem, seduced the woman and so mingled heresy with Christianity. Christ, the Sun, they say did not die and was not resurrected, and because of this they fast on Sunday. And St. Ephrem came and could not turn him away from his heresy and he cursed him and left.[54]

We see that the circumstances in which this Pōł(Paul) acts are completely different from the atmosphere that surrounded Paul, son of Kallinike, which is why the information from the Armenian story could not be derived from the Greek. However, it is quite possible that the chapter on Pōł in the *History* of Peter of Sicily is a distant reminiscence of the events connected with the son of Kallinike.

It must be underlined that, according to the sources, the Paulicians cursed Pōł but did not deny his existence. It is improbable that they would have denied so categorically an imaginary person. The very fact of such an attitude towards the founder of the sect is quite clear. The movement developed constantly and at its centre there arose various conflicts. The followers of Joseph-Epaphroditus disliked the followers of Zacharias. The followers of Sergius-Tychicus killed the disciples of Baanes. Subsequent followers of this movement could well have disliked and condemned its founder. Thus it may be supposed that the legend of the son of Kallinike is a reflection of real events. Paul is a historical person, he is the founder of the sect, although subsequently he was denounced. In an environment hostile to the heretics, he began to be called *Pawłik* from which derives the name *Pawłikeankʻ* – Paulicians. Only one circumstance can give rise to doubt; Kallinike preaches Manichaean doctrine at a time when there is nothing in common between Manichaeanism and Paulicianism. This may be an expression of the Orthodox writer's tendency once more to restate the doctrine of the official church, according to which the Paulicians are the same as the Manichaeans, and desire to trace back their foundation to a Manichaean environment. In any case the fact that the Greek writers accuse Kallinike of Manichaeanism cannot in itself serve as an argument against the historicity of her son.

To what period must the activity of the founder of the sect be assigned? In the sources there is no direct indication and the synchronisation of events with the history of the Paulicians is only possible from the time of Constantine-Silvanus, a contemporary of the emperor Constans II. However, along with many of the eighth century and later sources, in which the heretics are mentioned under the name Paulicians, a document from the middle of the sixth century has been preserved. This is the *Oath of Union* taken at the council of Dvin summoned by the kat'ołikos Nersēs II of Aštarak.[55] If the phrase in which the Paulicians are referred to is authentic, then the date for the origin of Paulicianism must be taken further back than the appearance of the *Oath of Union*.

In his discourse *Against the Paulicians*, Yovhannēs Ōjnec'i confirms that the heretics had already been reprimanded by the kat'ołikos Nersēs but had not been brought to reason and had gone into hiding. They were joined by the iconoclasts of Caucasian Albania. Before the arrival of the Arabs the heretics continued to live in hiding but later they became bolder and spread into the country. Before Yovhannēs Ōjnec'i, Armenia had had three kat'ołikoses with the name Nersēs; Nersēs I (died 374), Nersēs II of Aštarak [or Bagrewand] (548-557) and Nersēs III the Builder (641-661). The kat'ołikos Nersēs referred to by Ōjnec'i must be identified with one of these three. In 1900, Ter Mkrttschian published for the first time the text of the *Oath of Union* in which the Paulicians are mentioned in the form *Pawłikenac'* by Ōjnec'i. Hence the conclusion Garsoïan draws is that "there is no reason for doubting the authenticity of the *Oath of Union*, since it is found at its logical, chronological place in the compilation of the *Book of Letters*". The implication is that "we possess in Armenia an official record of the existence of Paulicians one century before the supposed organisation of the sect by Constantine-Silvanus, whom the Byzantine sources present as a contemporary of the emperor Constans II (641-668)."[56]

The authenticity of the document has been accepted by Armenian scholars.[57] However, there have also been some objections,[58] notably that of Bart'ikyan. His first objection is: "How could the sectarians referred to in the *Oath* be considered Paulicians who accept the sacrament of communion when there is evidence that the Paulicians rejected communion altogether."[59] There is no evidence that the Paulicians rejected the sacrament of communion. When it is said that the Paulicians rejected the Christian sacraments in general, the inference is that they regarded this and other orthodox sacraments as polluted. The Paulician objection to the sacrament of the communion amounts to a non-acceptance of the doctrine of Transubstantiation, that during the Holy Mass the bread and wine are transformed into the real Body and Blood of Christ. But what evidence has Bart'ikyan for suggesting that the Paulicians did not even accept the celebration of Christ's Last Supper, to which there is obvious reference in the allegation brought by the heretics that Christ's words "Take eat" are not uttered in relation to the communion but the practice of "common meals". The heresiarch Smbat Zarehawan also claimed that the utterance of Christ was not a reference to the Eucharist but to the custom of "communal meals". The evidence of the *Oath* "in the gathering of dedication [offering] of the Paulicians" is similarly a reference to this custom, by which the early Christians recalled the memory of Christ's Last Supper by organising *agapai*, the common religious meals, which seem to have been in use in the early Church in close relation to the Eucharist.[60] The words just preceding the above testimony "to bring the bread of offering to the place of their lawlessness"[61] affirms this beyond doubt.

A number of similar testimonies are to be found in the canons of the council of Partaw. "They built monasteries in the villages, so that the prelates could live there and the poor folk of the church. The blessed bread of dedication they take to the house of the priest and the elder brothers."[62] If it were just "bread offering" one would not attach great significance to it; but "the blessed bread of offering" refers to the custom of organising "common meals". It must be noted that this practice was widespread in the early church (1 Cor.II), particularly in the Nestorian Church, before it became extinct by the end of the seventh century. Evidence of it is to be found in the canons of the councils of Neocaesarea (early fourth century), Gangra (340-41), Laodicea, Partaw.[63]

Thus the evidence "dedication [offering] of the Paulicians" can be taken to mean that no gifts should be accepted from the Paulicians and no association should be established with them in general. Therefore one cannot base very far-reaching conclusions on the word "dedication" alone. Yuzbašyan is right in interpreting the passage from the *Oath of Union* as being a reference to the fact that the Paulicians believed in the symbolic and spiritual communion, understanding the bread and wine as symbolically representing the teaching of Christ.[64]

Bart'ikyan's second objection is that the Armenian sources are silent on the subject of the heretics for too long a period between the sixth and eighth centuries, if we accept the evidence of the *Oath of Union*, and that the next writer on the Paulicians, Yovhannēs Ōjnec'i, is insufficiently acquainted with Paulicianism, thus showing that the sect was newly established in Armenia in the eighth century. This argument is altogether unconvincing since it is based on the *a priori* assumption that the mention of the Paulicians is impossible in the late fifth century and indeed before the eighth century – an assumption that ignores the references to the sectarians in Vrt'anēs K'ert'oł, Yovhannēs Mayragomec'i and other sources. Bart'ikyan's criticism of Yovhannēs Ōjnec'i is also unwarranted. Yovhannēs Ōjnec'i recorded what he knew and his information is accurate, particularly in the case of the history of the Paulicians, which he traces back to the kat'ołikos Nersēs [II].

Bart'ikyan's last objection is that the mention of the name Paulicians in the *Oath of Union* is due to a copyist's error. In his opinion, the original reference was to Paulinians, followers of Paul of Samosata, and not Paulicians. The Armenian church, concludes Bart'ikyan, accused the Nestorians not of Paulicianism but of Paulianism, that is the heresy of the bishop of Antioch. First, if such a copyist's error occurred in Greek manuscripts it is no reason to believe that a similar error occurred in the Armenian manuscripts as well. Second, by Paulinians we understand the followers of Paul of Samosata. The church in A.D. 268 condemned Paul at a synod in Antioch. Thereafter he is mentioned and anathematized among the list of heretics (20 times in the *Book of Letters*), although his followers appear to have created a schism which lasted until the council of Nicaea. Their role in the Armenian church is insignificant. Third, any follower of Paul, whether of Paul the apostle or of any other Paul, in Armenian would be called *Pōłosean* and not Paulianist (see the Armenian translation of 1 Cor.1:12; 3:4). The most one would expect would be *Pōłoseank', Pōłoseanc'. Pawłianosk'*, as in *Nestorianosk'*. And lastly, in the Armenian version of the canons of the council of Nicaea the Greek name Paulianist [Παυλιανισταί] is translated *Pawłovnia* (in manuscript variants as *Pōłowniai, Pōłonari, Pawłonai*, etc), none of which is in the remotest way like the name Paulician.[65] Furthermore, the association of the Paulicians and Nestorians found in the *Oath of Union* is possible on historical grounds.

That Yovhannēs Ōjnec'i had in mind Nersēs II (584-557) agrees perfectly with the dating of the beginning of the movement suggested by the Greek sources. The relevant section of Yovhannēs Ōjnec'i's testimony reads:

> The remnant of the old Messalianism Paylakēnut'ean reprimanded by kat'ołikos Nersēs was not brought to reason after his death. They withdrew and hid in a certain locality of our country. They were joined by some iconoclasts denounced by the Albanian kat'ołikos and, until they found support in the precursors of an anti-Christ, they were afraid and feared the true and glorious religion of the Christians. But when they had the presumption to think that they had arrived at something important and new, in their treachery, they came bounding out of their lair and dared to penetrate into the interior of the country and inhabited regions.[66]

This evidence indicates that the Paulicians did take refuge in Armenia, that they were later joined and supported by the Albanian iconoclasts and that they found their allies among the precursors of anti-Christ, that is the Arabs. Let us try to date these events.

Information on the activities of the iconoclasts in Armenia and Albania is contained in the *History of the Caucasian Albanians* of Movsēs Dasxuranc'i, in chapter 46 of the second book, which also contains the epistle of Yovhannēs Mayragomec'i. There it is recorded:

> In the days when Lord Uxt'anēs (670-682), and after him Ełiazar, (628-688) directed the partiarchate of Albania, the land of Albania remained unaffected by the confusion and heresy which arose among both learned and ignorant men in many places . . . The news reached them, however, that certain people would not accept icons, while others would not practice baptism or bless the salt or impose the wedding crown in marriage, all by reason of the fact that the priesthood was

removed from the land. On account of these things Davit', bishop of *Mec Kołmank'*, wrote and asked Yovhan, an Armenian doctor, the cause of these matters, and he informed him accurately as follows: "This heresy appeared after the apostles, and iconoclasm first arose among the Greeks; on this account a great council was convened in Caesarea, which decreed that images were to be displayed in the house of God . . . Then a priest named Yesu, with T'adēos and Grigor, who were from Movsēs' See, left Dvin, went to the canton of Sotk' and began to preach saying: "Destroy all images painted in the churches and do not commune with worldly priests." Movsēs ordered them to return immediately, but they would not obey his command and left and took refuge in the province of Arc'ax. The iconoclasts who had descended upon Albania, however, polluted the country. Then the lord of Gardman seized the men and had them brought in chains to Armenia. They appeared before Yovhannēs Mayragomec'i who set them on the path of truth.[67]

It is apparently to these iconoclasts that Yovhannēs Ōjnec'i alludes in his treatise *Against the Paulicians*, for he speaks of the heretics who went into all parts of Armenia after the death of Nersēs, and were joined by certain iconoclasts pursued by the Albanians. We know for certain that Yovhannēs Mayragomec'i left Dvin and settled in Gardman in 633. The return of the heretics to Armenia occurred before that date, that is considerably earlier than the kat'ołikosate of Nersēs III (641-661). We are better informed of these events by a treatise ascribed to Vrt'anēs K'ert'oł, *Yałags Patkeramartic'*.[68] Der Nersessian, who has studied this source in detail, does not doubt that the statement of Yovhannēs Ōjnec'i refers to kat'ołikos Nersēs II (548-557) and that the Paulicians were joined by iconoclasts with whom Yovhannēs Mayragomec'i had dealings.[69]

Later the Paulicians found support among the Arabs. It is not easy to relate these vague testimonies to a definite period. Nevertheless, it is reasonable to suppose that it is an allusion to the period when the Armenians came into direct contact with the Arabs.

The Arab invasion of Armenia occurred in 640-42. In 652 an agreement was concluded between the commander of the Armenian troops, T'ēodor Řštuni, and Mu'āwiyah, which prescribed a light form of dependence on the caliphate. But in 654 the Arabs again pillaged the country and Ḥabīb ibn Maslama delivered to the population of Dvin, Christians, Jews and Zoroastrians, a letter of guarantee for their temples, goods and personal security. It is just in this period that the Paulicians may have found support in the shape of the Arabs, whose religious toleration is reflected in Ḥabīb's letter. Thus the first Armenian association with the Arabs falls in the period before the death of kat'ołikos Nersēs III (641-661), and once again the fact comes to mind that Yovhannēs Ōjnec'i was referring to Nersēs II (548-557).

Recognising the fact that the Paulicians were already known by the time of Nersēs II, we are obliged to give great credit to the reference to them in the *Oath of Union*. The analysis of this document on its own evidence shows that there is no reason to doubt its authenticity. Nor is there any doubt about dating it in the 24th year of the reign of Xosrov I Anuširvan (531-559), that is 554 or 555. In this document the Nestorians who came to Armenia on business from Xužastan are denounced. These Nestorians founded a monastery under the patronage of Manačrhi Ražik, and their missionaries brought men and wives of ignorant laymen to participate in their faith: "in the filth of their prayers to bring the bread of offering in the place of their impiety, to receive communion at their hands just as this is done in the gatherings of dedication [offering] of the Paulicians." As has been indicated above there is nothing extraordinary in the spelling of the form of the name *Pawłikenac'*; it is also found in other sources. As we have seen, there is no evidence that the Paulicians rejected communion altogether. The reference to the *Oath* is in relation to the ancient custom of organising "common meals", a practice also widespread among the Nestorians, which is also the basis for associating the two heresies.

The degree of truth in the legend of the sons of Kallinike can be disputed, but it is unfair to call it "evidence of Peter of Sicily's ignorance" (H. Grégoire) or "a legendary fabrication" (N. Garsoian). In adopting a critical attitude towards the sources written by the adversaries of the heretics, we must equally remember that the sources belonging to the heretics themselves are not free of tendentious opinions.

On the general history of the Paulician movement and its relation to and influence on other sects, the primary sources provide ample evidence and information. But there is no study devoted to the question of the organisation of the sect. This neglect is due to the lack of information in the primary sources. The interest of writers who were opposed to the movement was limited in regard to the organisation of the sect. However, in their writings there are scanty references which throw some light on this particular aspect of the movement. Particularly important in this respect are the *History* of Peter of Sicily, in which the chronological history of the Paulician movement is recorded from the beginning until 869, and the work of Patriarch Photius, *A History of the Manichaeans*, by which he understood the Paulicians.

The material which sheds some light on the organisation of the movement is from the ninth century, the period when it had gained the widest support and was so strong from a military point of view that the government of Byzantium had to take it into account very seriously. First, on the matter of the leadership of the sect: as a rule the heresiarch, or head of the group, was a single individual. However, the sources indicate that there were times when two names appeared in the leadership. The sources refer to such times only when controversy and struggle had arisen due to the emergence of two leaders. The first period was in the first half of the eighth century, when the sect was led by the two sons of the Armenian Paul Genesius-Timothy and Theodotus, who survived the systematic persecution under Justinian II. Between these two there was evidently serious controversy. In all probability Genesius proved to be victorious for he alone is mentioned in the sources thereafter. The movement was governed by two leaders for a second time during the ninth century by Sergius (801-835) and Baanes.

Was it then a common procedure to elect two heresiarchs? Patriarch Photius writes explicitly that after the death of Sergius, the sectarians "did not give the title *fighter of God* to either one or two."[70]

But despite this direct allusion of Photius to two heresiarchs, the conclusion to be drawn is merely that the movement was divided. It is natural that a movement which drew supporters in large numbers both from the city and from the countryside would be diversified, and internal hostility would have been unavoidable. This was clearly manifested during the first half of the ninth century when Sergius and Baanes were leaders. After Joseph-Epaphroditus's death, there was a contest over the succession and the Paulician community split into two factions. Joseph's immediate successor, Baanes was Armenian, but the victor, Sergius-Tychius, was an east Roman whose birthplace was a village in the theme of Armeniakon. According to Peter of Sicily, Baanes claimed that he, Baanes, had remained faithful to the doctrine that had been transmitted to him by Joseph, whereas "You, Sergius, are a newcomer who has never seen any of our teachers or kept company with them."[71] Sergius, however, was obdurate, and "split the sect in two".[72]

Although the source accuses Sergius of dividing the movement into two parties, one under his leadership and the other under that of Baanes, in all probability the division in the sect existed before the emergence of the two heresiarchs. Each waged a fierce struggle against the other in order to weaken the other party and to attract its supporters to his side. Peter of Sicily testifies that Sergius reacted violently and radically against Baanes in order to win the support of "Orthodox Christians".[73] It is not easy to see why the Orthodox Christians would have chosen to support Sergius (which meant becoming sectarians themselves) when the hostility was between the two heresiarchs. But their motives are sufficiently explained by Photius. Photius stresses that during this period of hostility Sergius was trying to disrupt and discount the other party.[74] This hostility continued even after the death of Sergius (835). The sources record that Sergius's partisans were thirsting to massacre Baanes's partisans as if they were of "another faith"(*ὡς ἑτεροπίστους παντελῶς*).[75] One of the disciples of Sergius tried to restrain them by reminding them that before Sergius came "we all held one faith".[76] But according to the source the followers of Sergius fought the Baanites in order to clear themselves of the disrepute they had suffered because of their enemies.[77]

As shown above, the leaders of the movement were elected, but it must be observed that not all the sectarians participated in the election procedure. The heresiarch was elected by the inner circle of the sect, whose members were known as the *synekdemoi.*[78] Peter of Sicily records that, after the death of Sergius, the *synekdemoi* and the rest of the sectarians did not elect any heresiarch. Photius, however, states the reason for this in more specific terms. He writes that after the death of Sergius the *synekdemoi* "did not give the title 'fighter of God' to either one or two".[79] The *synekdemoi* in their turn elected and appointed the *μιερεῖς* called the *notaries* (*νοτάριος*). The latter had the responsibility of propagating the Paulician doctrine.[80]

Besides these two major groupings, the heresiarch also had a group of disciples called *astatoi* (ἄστατοι).[81] The information the sources supply on these people is very scanty; but it appears that while the two former groups were responsible for missionary work, the *astatoi* organised and planned the strategy of conflict against the Paulician's adversaries. The sources only mention the fact that the *astatoi* planned the plot against the Byzantine governor of Neocaesarea, Parakondakes, and the bishop of the same city, Thomas. Both these victims were appointed by Byzantium to the Armeniakon theme to investigate Sergius's activities.

Another crucial aspect of the Paulician movement is the question of their military organisation. For the investigation of this particular problem the work of Patriarch Photius is indispensable. Photius demonstrates that the Paulicians, from the beginning of the ninth century if not earlier, had armies commanded not, as might be expected, by the heresiarch but by a military official. Photius refers to him as the "ruler of the armed forces" (τῆς ὁπλιτικῆς δυνάμεως ὁ ἄρχων).[82] It appears that he had considerable influence and could have played a very important role in the internal affairs of the sect. Photius points out that Sergius and his followers were in a stronger position than his opponent Baanes, not only in terms of numbers, but also because the leader of the armed forces was a convinced supporter of Sergius:

> Ἐπεκράτει γὰρ ἡ μερὶς Σεργίου τῷ τε πλήθει καὶ ὅτι τῆς ἐν αὐτοῖς ὁπλιτικῆς δυνάμεως ὁ ἄρχων τῇ δόξῃ προσαπέκλινεν Σεργίου, καὶ ἂν εἷς.[83]

This may be thought to lead to the conclusion that in the Paulician organisation there was a specific division of duties between the heresiarch and the military leader. The heresiarch was responsible for organising and waging religious warfare while the commander had specifically military responsibility. This strict differentiation of duties has a historical background. In the ninth century the Paulicians, alongside their missionary activities, carried out very effective military campaigns. It was the emperor Constantine V (740-775) who supported and used Paulicians to consolidate his iconoclastic policies. He transferred great numbers of Paulicians from the eastern provinces, notably from Armenia, and settled them in Constantinople and in Thrace. The Paulicians were so strong and so widespread at this time, and were so important from a military point of view, that the government in Byzantium had to take them into account very seriously. When in the ninth century Byzantium resumed its persecution of its Paulician subjects, the Paulicians, under the leadership of their two most successful military leaders, staged their counter offensives.

According to Peter of Sicily, the disciples of Sergius did not appoint any other heresiarch after their master's death, as had been done in the past: μηκέτι ἕνα διδάσκαλον ἀνακηρύξαντες καθάπερ οἱ πρώην.[84] He does, however, record that after Sergius, Karbeas became the leader of the sect.[85] He was only a military leader. If Photius had not recorded the fact that in the Paulician community two leaders existed we would have to regard the evidence of Peter of Sicily, that the *synekdemoi* did not elect any heresiarch after the death of Sergius, as being inaccurate or that the election of

Karbeas went against this policy. But Photius elucidates the role played by Karbeas: he was the leader only of the armed forces (*δυνάμεως ὁ ἄρχων*).

This is confirmed by other evidence found in Photius but lacking in Peter of Sicily. According to Photius, Karbeas was totally indifferent to matters of faith (*πίστιν μὲν οὐδ' ἥντινα στέργων*),[86] a statement which could never have been made in relation to the conduct of the religious leader. This also explains why in all the abjuration formulae, which contain specific accusations against the Paulician spiritual leaders, the names of Karbeas and his successor, John Chrysocheir, are missing when all the other heresiarchs are mentioned.[87]

The Paulician community had its religious heresiarch who was elected by the *synekdemoi*[88] and its military leader who was elected by all the community. There is no means of knowing how far the military leader was subject to the religious leader, but the evidence suggests that the military leader was completely independent. The *synekdemoi* were subject to the heresiarch who, like the *notaries*, was concerned only with the doctrinal and religious aspects of the Paulician movement. The *astatoi* were also subordinate to the heresiarch and were particularly concerned with social problems.

CHAPTER III

ARMENIA IN THE EIGHTH AND NINTH CENTURIES: A SOCIAL, ECONOMIC AND POLITICAL SURVEY

The situation in Asia at the death of Heraclius (610-41) was very discouraging for Byzantium. The waves of Arabs emerging from the peninsula swept into the once mighty Persian empire, and occupied its territories piecemeal. Meanwhile the religious policy of Heraclius had widened the rift between Armenia and Byzantium. Every Byzantine military intervention in Armenia, in the course of the struggle against the advance of the Arabs, invariably entailed a rather cavalier Imperial imposition of the faith of Chalcedon on its population. The Byzantine intolerance partly accounts for the startling rapidity and ease with which the Arab armies occupied Syria, Palestine and Armenia. In the words of Bar-Hebraeus "these Ismaelites conquered us by divine providence in the days of Heraclius and they freed us from the hands of the Greeks".[1]

The history of the conquest of Armenia by the Arabs presents in its details many uncertainties and obscurities, for the information found in Arabic, Armenian and Greek sources is often contradictory. H. Manandyan[2] who has submitted the traditional data to close criticism arrived at the conclusion that until 650 there had been three Arab invasions: (i) in 640, the first invasion through the Tarōn region and the capture of Dvin on 6th October 640;(ii) in 642-43, the second invasion by way of Ādharbāydjān into Persarmenia; (iii) in 650, the third invasion carried out from Ādharbāydjān and marked by the taking of Arcapʻ in the Kogovit district to the north-east of Lake Van on 8th August 650. These invasions were not conquering expeditions but merely disorderly raids. Only the invasion of 654 can be considered as a true conquest, and it is consequently the only expedition which is recorded in detail in Arabic sources, while the three earlier raids are known to us essentially through Armenian sources.

Initially the relationship between Armenia and the Caliphate was based for the most part on the treaty concluded in 652 between Muʻ āwiyah and Tʻēodor Řštuni. The terms of the agreement, as recorded by Sebēos, were that the Arabs should refrain from posting governors or garrisons in Armenia, that they should come to Armenia's aid in the event of an attack on her, and that the Armenians, on their side were bound to pay only light tribute to the Caliphate and to send a supporting army to the Arabs in times of need. In addition to this treaty, a guarantee of safety and religious toleration was granted to the Armenian church: "This is the treaty of Ḥabīb ibn-Maslama with the Christians, Magians and the Jews of Dabīl [Dvin], including those present and absent. I have granted you safety for your lives, possessions, churches, places of worship, and the city wall. Thus you are safe and we are bound to fulfil our covenant, so long as you fulfil yours and pay poll-tax and *kharādj*. Thereunto Allah is witness and it suffices to have Him for witness".[3]

This indicates that in the seventh century the Caliphate had no representative, whether administrative or military in Armenia, and the country enjoyed a degree of independence such as it had not known since the fall of the Arsacids. The period of Arab domination in Armenia was characterised by certain privileges which distinguished it from the previous Perso-Byzantine era. The natural policy of both the Persians and Byzantines toward Armenia had been to bind the country to themselves by various religious and political ties. In the *ostikanate* of Armīniya, which included Armenia proper, Albania and eastern Iberia (Kart'li) the kat'ołikos was a political figure and the head of the church. Next in importance came the *naxarars*, the heads of the princely houses. Their hereditary patrimonial domains constituted autonomous principalities over which they exercised absolute military, judicial and administrative powers. The Armenian *naxarars* were able to hold important offices such as *sparapet* (chief of armies), *hazarapet* (general administrator of the realm) without abandoning their religion. The next group in the hierarchic order was formed by the *azats* (the freemen), owners of small fiefs, and vassals of the *naxarars*. The majority of the common people (*ṙamik*) consisted of peasants. They were serfs, attached to the soil, which they tilled for the benefit of their masters, retaining only a small part of the products for their own use. They could own their house and a few animals, but most of them lived in great poverty.

The taxation policies of the Caliphate in Armenia from A.D. 652 to 862 were subject to a number of changes as regards the amount and method of collection. We can distinguish five periods.[4]

(i) From the beginning of the invasions up to the treaty with Mu'āwiyah I (640-652).

(ii) From Mu'āwiyah I to caliph 'Abd al-Malik (685-705).

(iii) 'Abd al-Malik till the time of caliph Ḥishām (724-743).

(iv) From Ḥishām till the end of the Umayyad dynasty (724-750).

(v) The 'Abbāsid period (750-862).

Under the Umayyads, particularly in the early period, Arab exploitation of the population was relatively mild and bearable. The reasons for this were twofold. First, because Armenia accepted the rule of the Arab Caliphate, on the definite condition that she would keep her internal autonomy and her *naxarar* structure. Armenia never lost its internal autonomy, and this is well illustrated by al-Balādhurī, who drew a careful distinction between the general term "Armīniya" and the specific "Armaniyākus", governed by an Armenian prince, who was subject to the Ostikan of "Armīniya" but was in full control of the internal government.[5] Second, this cautious policy can be explained by the great strategic and military importance of Armenia, which the Arabs wished to make use of to protect their new frontiers against Byzantium. Even in this period, however, Arab domination was ruinous for Armenia. During the periodic wars between the Caliphate and Byzantium, Armenia repeatedly changed her allegiance and was mercilessly devastated by both sides. Dionysios of Tell-Mahrē, describing the campaign of the Arab general Maslama against Byzantium in A.D. 716-717 and his appearance in the interior of Armenia, says: "This entire country was noted for its innumerable inhabitants, many vineyards, fields of grain, and all kinds of magnificent trees. From that time, it became empty and no population is left in her provinces."[6]

If in the first and second periods Armenia was devastated as a result of the Arab-Byzantine wars on her territory, in the third period of Arab rule, Armenia was drained by the burden of heavy and unbearable taxation, which then provoked general revolts. According to Samuēl of Ani, the Caliphate at the time of its consolidation in Armenia "took from each household four dirhams, three modii of sifted wheat, one hempen rope and one gauntlet. From priests, however, as from the *azats* and the knights, it was ordered to levy no taxes."[7]

The tax policy of the Caliphate in Armenia underwent a radical change in the time of the caliph Ḥishām (724-743). In 724-725 a general census of men, cattle, and lands was taken in Armenia. All tax privileges in autonomous Armenia were revoked and taxes were levied, not from households, as formerly, but per person, and according to the quantity of landed property. In this way the new system of poll tax, tax on cattle, and land tax was introduced. The Armenian historian Movsēs Dasxuranc'i[8] writes:

> In the summer of the year 174 of the Armenian era, there was a plague among the cattle, and in the winter a cadaster was made by Hert which subjected man and beast and all regions of the country to servitude by the imposition of heavy tribute.[9]

Even before this general census, the caliph Yazīd II (720-724) appointed al-Djarrah ibn al-Ḥakam governor of Armenia and new weights and measures were introduced by him. Al-Balādhurī reports:

> After him [Hert], al-Djarrah ibn Abdullah al-Ḥakam of the Mashidj tribe was appointed governor of Armenia. When he came to Berday he was informed of the abuses in the local weights and measures and he eliminated them by introducing a new and exact measure known as the Djarrahid one, which is in use even today among the population.[10]

The imposition of unbearable taxation was accompanied by brutal exploitation and pillage. There is interesting evidence of this in al-Balādhurī in regard to fishing rights in Lake Van:

As for lake Tirrih, he [Ḥabīb ibn Maṣlama] did not touch it and it remained free until the time when Muḥammad ibn Marwān became governor of Djazīra and Armenia. He laid hands on the entire catch and sold it, deriving a great profit therefrom. After him, the lake passed to Muḥammad ibn Marwān from whom it was later taken.[11]

Łewond writes that 'Abd al-'Azīz, who was governor of Armenia under the caliph al-Wallīd (705-715), was more benevolent, for "when he became the governor of our land of Armenia he pacified her by protecting her from all unjustified attacks and by stern reproofs subdued the haughty arrogance of the sons of Isma'īl."[12]

The tax policy of the Caliphate in Armenia during the last period (750-862) dealt heavy blows to the Armenian economy, causing a regression in the social life of Armenia, accompanied by financial and economic collapse.

The Abbāsid dynasty, deprived of all its revenues from its African colonies, transferred the burden of taxation to the eastern provinces. Thus, according to Qudāma[13], during the reign of caliph al-Mu'taṣim (833-842) the budget of the empire was 388 million dirhams, and twenty years later during the reign of caliph al-Mutawakkil (847-861) it rose to 960 million. According to Łewond, at the time of the caliph al-Manṣūr (754-755) Armenia was unable to pay the taxes to the 'Abbāsids in currency because of the lack of silver and other precious metals in the country.[14] The people were selling their possessions at derisory prices and could not raise the sum needed for the taxes. According to Michael the Syrian, in northern Mesopotamia the people were giving their children away to the tax-collectors for five dirhams[15], when oxen and asses were for sale there for one dirham.

Łewond gives us another indirect indication of the reasons for the lack of money and the decline of monetary relations:

> . . . and after him his son al-Mahdī inherited. He was more benevolent than his father and of better nature. He opened all the treasuries which godless Abdul had kept locked and distributed pay to his troops. He abolished frontier duty so as to give merchants the possibility of trading and of satisfying the poor. Prosperity appeared in the land, the extraction of silver increased and the inhabitants rested from the coercion of taxes . . . as a result of the discovery of silver our country rested from the cruel evils of poverty.[16]

The Armenian revolt of 774 was a direct consequence of these brutalities. After a short period of relaxation on the accession of Hārūn al-Rashīd, the Caliphate reverted to its old policies. The Armenian sources speak in very grim terms about the socio-economic conditions in Armenia during the 'Abbāsid period. The Arab sources are more precise.

Ibn Khaldūn (1332-1406) in his *Prolegomena* gives a list of revenues from the provinces, where he mentions payment in kind as well as monetary tribute from Armenia:[17]

13,000,000 dirhams
Embroidered carpets: 20
Variegated cloth (*raqm*): 580 pieces
Salted *sūrmâhî* fish: 10,000 pounds
Herring (ṭarîkh): 10,000 pounds
Mules: 200
Falcons: 30

The list of revenues from the provinces prepared by Abu'l-Wazīr 'Umar ibn al-Mutarrif in the early part of the reign of Hārūn al-Rashīd has a special importance in the fiscal and administrative history of Islam. It is the second list of revenues from the provinces belonging to the 'Abbāsid Caliphate. It contains, too, details about the revenues in kind which were sent from the provinces to Baghdad, the capital of the Arab empire from A.D. 762. A second list has been preserved in a unique manuscript by Muḥammad ibn 'Abdūs al-Djahshiyāri, preserved in the Nationalbibliothek in Vienna. A. Kremer analysed it in his article *Über das Budget der Einnahmen unter der Regierung des Hārūn al-Rashīd.*[18]

Al-Djahshiyāri says that his list was written during the reign of Hārūn al-Rashīd. In general, Ibn Khaldūn's list resembles that of Djahshiyāri (d.942). The identity of the lists of Djahshiyāri and Ibn Khaldūn convinced von Kremer that Ibn Khaldūn's list was a version of Djahshiyāri's list, and that it represented the revenue in the time of Hārūn al-Rashīd (786-809). In the Arabic manuscript the letter "A" has been erased from the name "Armīniya" and scholars have taken it to be a reference to Urmiya and not Armenia. This is the interpretation given by R. Levy[19], but von Kremer suggested that it should read "Armenia". In the manuscript, the letter "n" is not erased, so that if Levy were consistent he should have read *Armena* or *Urmina*, but not Urmiya.

Thirteen million dirhams was most probably the highest limit ever reached during the first period of 'Abbāsid rule under caliph Manṣūr and Hārūn al-Rashīd. It is enough to compare the taxes of the 'Abbāsid period with those of the Umayyad period to see the apparent increase. According to the Arab geographers Khurradādhbih and Qudāma, Armenia paid only 4 million dirhams[20] when the Umayyads were in power. This sharp increase in the monetary payment was not just a result of high taxes, but was due to the fact that monetary payments were far more important under the 'Abbāsid dynasty.

Another manuscript, which exists in the Auqāf library at the Bibliothèque Générale in Rabat (No.199)[21] is by Khalīfa Ibn Khayyāṭ, and gives another summarised estimate of the treasury receipts for a year during the reign of Hārūn al-Rashīd. The list resembles that of Djahshiyāri in the names and order of the provinces, but there are numerous differences between the two lists. The minor differences in the figures of the lists of Djahshiyāri and Ibn Khaldūn suggest that they were derived from one original source, the wider differences suggest that the latter presents an estimate of the revenues for a year different from that of the list of Djahshiyāri. The fact that

Khalīfa's text states positively that the estimate of his list was submitted two years after the accession of Hārūn al-Rashīd, while Djahshiyāri states that his list was compiled at the time of Hārūn al-Rashīd, may favour this assumption. The list is as follows:

Armenia:

12 million dirhams
20 red carpets
600 pieces of cloth

When Ašot Bagratuni became "prince of princes" and later king, Armenia continued to pay an annual tribute to the 'Abbāsid Caliphate. Ibn-Ḥawkal's *Kitāb al-masālik wa'l-mamālik*[22] contains a list of the Armenian and Arrān (Albanian) princes who paid an annual tribute to the Caliphate, through the Arab princes in Atrpatakan:

> As regards the situation obtaining (in Armenia) – so far as I could ascertain – its contributions (*jibāyāt*) and the tributes imposed on the (vassal) kings of the marches (*mulūk al-aṭrāf*), clearly explain the position of the region and point to the correctness of its description. Although at times (the tribute) increased or decreased, the average of what was contributed and the highest standard of what was levied from (the region) in the year 344/955, by virtue of the agreements (*muwāqafāt*) which Abul-Qāsim 'Alī b. Ja'far, (a former) steward (*ṣāḥib al-zimām*) of Abul-Qāsim Yūsuf b. Abil-Sāj, effected on behalf of Marzubān b. Muḥammad, whose vazir he (later) was were as follows:
>
> (1) He (Marzubān) agreed with Muḥammad b. Aḥmad al-Azdī, lord of Sharvān-shāh [*sic*] and its king, for a payment of 1,000,000 dirhams.
>
> (2) Ishkhānīq, lord of Shakkī, known as Abū 'Abd al-Malik, also entered (*dakhala*) into an agreement with him.
>
> (3) He agreed with Sanḥārīb, known as Ibn Sawāda, lord of al-Rub', for a sum of 300,000 dirhams, and some additional offerings (*alṭāf*).
>
> (4) (Similarly) the lord of Jurz, Vashagān b. Mūsā – 200,000 dirhams.
>
> (5) He agreed with Abul-Qāsim al-Wayzūrī, lord of Wayzūr (Vayoc' jor) for 50,000 dinārs and offerings.
>
> (6) (Similarly) Abul-Hayja b. Rawwād, from his districts in Ahr and Varzuqan – 50,000 dinārs and offerings.
>
> (7) (Similarly) Abul-Qāsim al-Jydhānī from his districts and (on account of) the arrears (*baqāyā*) due from them – 400,000 dirhams, but he wanted (this sum) to be diminished and was importunate in (his) begging; therefore, in spiteful reaction (*tabarrum*) to his behaviour, the sum was increased by another 300,000 dirhams and 100 cuts of Rūmī brocade.
>
> (8) He (Marzubān) bound over (*alzama*) the sons of al-Dayrānī to pay according

to the (previously) agreed (sum), 100,000 dirhams yearly, but exempted them from payment for four years, in recompense for their having surrendered to him Daysam b. Shādhlūya, who had sought their protection but whom they betrayed.

(9) He agreed with the sons of Sunbāṭ, with regard to their districts in Inner Armenia, for 2,000,000 dirhams . . . but afterwards remitted 200,000 dirhams.

(10) He agreed with Sanḥārīb, lord of Khachen, for 100,000 dirhams, and offerings and horses (to the value of) 50,000 dirhams.

The tributes in gold and silver, with supplements (*tawābi'*) and offerings consisting of mules, horses, and ornaments (*ḥuliyy*) amounted to 10,000,000 dirhams.

Of the ten vassals mentioned in the text, six are Armenian kings. The "sons of Sunbāṭ" are the Bagratids Ašot and Abas, sons of Smbat I (890-914). In the same manner "sons of al-Dayrānī" are the rulers of Vaspurakan of the Arcruni family. In 955 the ruling prince was Abu Sahl Hamazasp (953-972), who succeeded his brother Derenik Ašot (937 - 953). Both were grandsons of Grigor Derenik (847 - 886). "Sanḥārib b. Sawada" is Yovhannēs Senek'erim, Lord of P'arisos. "Vashaqān ibn Mūsā" is the son of the rebellious governor of Uti, Movsēs[23], against whom Ašot II led an expedition in 929.[24]

This estimate of Ibn Ḥawḳal was composed in A.D. 955 and reflects the situation of the period of Abas (928-953), when the Armenian kingdom was paying tribute to the rulers of Atrpataken.

The disintegration of the Caliphate and a gradual strengthening of the Byzantine Empire was taking place during the second half of the ninth century. Under Basil I (867-886), Byzantium took advantage of the new situation and destroyed the fortified positions of the Arabs. In 872 Tephrike, the Paulician stronghold, was destroyed by Basil I. After this event the Byzantines could operate freely against the line of defence and they penetrated step by step into the provinces between Malaṭya and eastern Cilicia by capturing the almost inaccessible fortified posts of the Arabs. In the reign of Romanus Lecapenus (920-944) Byzantium continued the attack with success.

With the downfall of the Caliphate under al-Muḳtadir (908-932), an event unheard of for more than a century occurred: the iron ring of fortifications was pierced by the Armeno-Byzantine general Ioannes Kourkouas. The Greeks took Malaṭya in 926; in 927 they overran Armenia as far as the capital, Dvin; in 928 they occupied the western part of the country to Theodosiopolis and in 929, northern Mesopotamia between Mayyāfāriḳīn, Amida (Diyārbakr) and Malaṭya. Although the Arab governors, operating from Mosul and Tarsus, made repeated attempts to repel Kourkouas's army, they were not successful. In 934, Samosata and western Armenia were lost to Islam.[25] In Armenia also a national revival had taken place, gathering momentum during the ninth century under the Bagratids, who in A.D. 884 restored the Armenian monarchy. The outstanding figure was the Bagratid prince Ašot. By remaining faithful to the Caliphate and neutral during the wars of Basil I, Ašot remained "prince of princes" for twenty-five years, until, in A.D. 887-889, he received from the caliph al-Mu'tamid a crown and the title of king *Malik al-Arman.*[26] This title was also recognised by the emperor Basil I[27], and thus Byzantium seemed to accept the solution of maintaining a protectorate rather than of annexation.[28]

The flourishing situation in Armenia in the Bagratid period is evident from the fact that contemporary Arab writers considered her one of the richest lands of the Caliphate. This is also confirmed by the Armenian sources. For instance, Asołik testifies that: "In the days of Smbat I and in those of his father's rule, peace reigned everywhere in our land, and each one, in the words of the prophet, dwelt safely under his vine and under his fig tree. The fields became settlements and the settlements cities in their population and wealth, so that even the shepherds began to appear in silken garments."[29]

The important factor in the testimony is that at this period small settlements expanded and became "cities in their population and wealth".[30] The historian Yovhannēs Drasxanakertc'i gives a vivid description of the welfare of Armenia under Smbat (890-913/4):

> And in these days the Lord showed benevolence to our land of Armenia, he defended her and favoured her in all good undertakings. At that time all dwelt in their inherited possessions, and having appropriated the land, they set out vineyards and planted olive trees and gardens, they ploughed up fields among the thorns and gathered a harvest hundredfold. The barns were filled with wheat after the harvest and the cellars were filled with wine after the gathering of the grapes. The mountains rejoiced since the herds of cattle and flocks of sheep multiplied on them. Our chief *naxarars*, feeling themselves safe and free from plundering raids, built stone churches in isolated spots, villages and settlements.[31]

The historian Aristakēs Lastiverc'i, a contemporary of both the splendour and the fall of the capital Ani, has left us a picture of the kingdom of Ani before the invasion of the Seljuqs: "Its nobles in their gorgeous costumes and glittering array of armour and equipment, held sway in their baronial seats; the people danced and sang merry songs, the sounds of the flute, cymbals and other instruments gladdened the air . . . ".[32]

Industries and commerce flourished, participating in two great economic systems, the Caspian of the Muslims and the Pontic of the Byzantines. Old cities revived, new ones, like Ani, arose. The systematic excavations of Ani made by Marr[33] gave abundant material for the reconstruction of the cultural and economic life of this great trade centre, with its industrial life, the products of which were exported abroad. Weaving, dyeing and embroidery were the chief industries of the Armenian economy. In his work, *The Book of Roads and Realms*, Iṣṭakhrī writes that, "Dabīl [Dvin] is greater than Ardabil . . . In this town are made woollen garments and rugs, cushions, seats, laces and other items of Armenian manufacture. From them is also obtained the dye named *ḳirmiz* and cloth is dyed with it. I learned that it is a worm which weaves around itself a cocoon similar to that of the silk worm. In addition to this I learned that many silken cloths are manufactured there."[34]

Another Arab geographer, Ibn Ḥawḳal, adds the following: "In Dabīl are made many silken garments. As for these last there are many like them in the land of Rūm, although these are more valuable. And as for the items called "Armenian weaving" they are seats, rugs, covers and cushions. There is none equal to them among the things of this world from end to end, and in all directions."[35] These references mention the cloths of Dvin known under the name of *marizi*, and the multicoloured flowered silken cloth called *bozjun*. The textiles of Armenia were exported to the eastern provinces of the Caliphate and to Byzantium. Von Kremer concluded that in Trebizond, the main port of international trade, excellent Armenian silken cloths such as *dybag* and *bozjun*, as well as other cloths, were for sale.[36] Evidence for the existence of rich garments worked with patterns and figures can be found in the work of Yovhannēs[37], in the summary revenue estimates of the Caliphate, and in excavations in Ani in 1908.[38]

We learn from a reference by Łewond that a silver mine was discovered in the mountains of Armenia in the last quarter of the eighth century. When speaking of the heavy monetary tribute under the early 'Abbāsid dynasty, and the poverty-stricken condition of Armenia, caused by the deficiency of currency, Łewond testifies that the mining of silver in these mountains helped to a great extent to avert an acute monetary crisis. Ibn Ḥawḳal, in his *Book of Roads and Realms*, says that natron was obtained in the vicinity of Lake Van and exported to al-Irāk. Near the same lake were to be found mines of arsenic which was exported to the same countries.[39] According to Ibn al-Faḳih , mountain resin, mercury, copper sulphate, silver and lead were found in Armenia.[40] Movsēs Dasxuranc'i speaks of master craftsmen having knowledge of working gold, of the production of silver and iron, and of the smelting of copper.[41]

The *ṭarīkh* fish of Lake Van and the fish of the Kura and Araxes rivers in particular are often mentioned by Arab writers as important items of export.[42] In this connection the city of Berday was important, for the Arab historian al-Muḳaddasī calls it the Baghdad of that region: "From Berday are exported covers and there one also finds excellent mules . . . nothing can be compared to the skins, carpets, and dyes made there, to the fruit called *žukal*, and to the fish *ṭarīkh*."[43] In the tax list of Ibn Khaldūn and others we notice the mention of other important items of export: rugs, carpets, horses, etc.

According to the Byzantine writer Michael Attaliates[44], Arcn, founded near the abandoned and empty Theodosiopolis, was a large unfortified city with a convenient location, and in it goods brought from Persia, India and the rest of Asia, changed hands. The Byzantine chronicler Cedrenus wrote:

> Arcn was an open and very rich city with a very large population. Local merchants lived here and a large number of Syrians, Armenians and other peoples. Taking strength from their number they did not find it necessary to live within walls despite the proximity of Theodosiopolis, a large and strong city with impregnable fortifications.[45]

The Armenian historian Aristakēs Lastiverc'i wrote about the wealth of the cities accumulated through trade: "wondrous and famed city of Arcn into which wealth poured by land and sea".[46] Describing the city of Kars, Aristakēs noted the wealth of the inhabitants of the city, and underlined once more that their riches were accumulated "from the sea and land". These testimonies confirm that the newly re-established international trade was the main source of the wealth of the Armenian towns. The foreign trade of Byzantium with the Orient was the dominant factor in Armenian economic life and provided the means for the swift rise of her cities.

The increase in material wealth in the country, and the accumulation of considerable monetary wealth in the hands of the feudal nobility and of the church, created exceptionally favourable circumstances for building activities. Architecture entered a new flourishing phase as Caucasian dynasts vied with one another in building monasteries and castles, palaces, hostelries, and underground water conduits like the one that brought water from the summit of mount Varag to Ani. The buildings were richly decorated, judging from the description of T'ovma Arcruni. Although these have been destroyed, there still remain several monastic ensembles, like those of Sanahin and Hałbat, built during the reign of Ašot III (952-977) in the north, and Tat'ev in the province of Siwnik'.[73] Nowhere is this better seen than in the churches and public buildings in the Bagratid capital Ani. Among the noteworthy churches of this period are the cathedral of Ani, the church of St. Grigor, the exquisite Shepherd's chapel and the church of Ałt'amar, built on a small island situated south-east of Lake Van, all of which unquestionably needed enormous wealth.[47]

In the tenth and eleventh centuries, as is clearly witnessed by Armenian inscriptions, a shift was taking place from the obligations in kind of the peasants to a system of monetary payments. From the account of Lastiverc'i this process of broad extension of a monetary economy was accompanied by unhealthy manifestations, brought about by the growing role of usurious capital and the brutal exploitation of the lower classes of the population.

"The love for silver was highly commended instead of love for God and Christ".[48] In his description of the pillage of the city of Arcn (1049), Aristakēs Lastiverc'i relates that:

> A law on growth and percentage and surtax on grain was set up here; the land is polluted by this and at the present time impediments are set in the way of those bringing the fruits of the earth to feed the people. He who deceives his friend boasts that he is wise and he who robs says that he is mighty. The wealthy have seized the houses of their relatives and the boundaries of their fields.[49]

There was growing discontent among the people and a sharp decline in the free peasantry as a result of this exploitation. The large landowners and feudal magnates tried to absorb the holdings of the small proprietors; when villages were bought either by the feudal lords or by the monasteries, the peasants were often reduced to serfdom. In the province of Siwnik' the peasants of several villages which had been bought by the monastery of Tat'ev revolted more than once. They refused to cede their lands, and attacked the monastery.[50] The same author, speaking of the capture and destruction of the city of Ani (1064), noted particularly the presence of usury and social unrest:

> Because of the excess of injustice which took place in it, a mighty and beautiful palace was burned down and all of its buildings were reduced to a heap of earth, and the licentiousness and evil which had occurred in it came to an end. This is the lot of unjust cities which are built on the blood of others and which grow rich at the expense of the homeless, of those who toil by the sweat of their brow, they build their houses on luxury and the infringement of right, they seek for themselves pleasure and profit having no pity in their souls for the poor and the homeless, withdrawing not from evil deeds, because they are possessed by their passions.[51]

The Armenian historian, Matt'ēos Uṙhayec'i gives us information concerning the enormous wealth in the hands of the clergy. The kat'ołikos Petros (1019-1059) "had estates given to him by the Armenian kings, 500 villages, large profitable settlements"[52] and, as Lastiverc'i confirms "he was extremely fond of wealth".[53] At the time of the taking of the city of Arcn by the Seljuq generals, Matt'ēos writes that ". . . the treasures of the chorepiscopos Dawt'uk were seized by Ibrāhīm. His treasures were loaded on forty camels. From his house eight hundred ploughs with six pairs of oxen apiece went forth for the ploughing."[54]

The oppressive economic yoke borne by the working population is also indicated by the fact that we have references to peasant uprisings in this period. Yovhannēs kat'ołikos writes:

> the lower classes wished to be more competent than the upper class, and the servants planned, Solomon-like, how their masters should wear sandals and go on foot and how they themselves should sit on magnificent and prancing horses. They became proud, insolent and raised a great rebellion.[55]

The religious and social discourses of Aristakēs Lastiverc'i on the good old days, and his complaints as to the greed and love of gain of the ruling classes and the growth of usury, the concentration of the possessions and the lands of the poor in the hands of the rich, may serve as indications of the shift which had taken place in the economic life of Armenia[56], and which resulted in a worsening of social conflict in the tenth and eleventh centuries and growing discontent among the people:

> The heretical sect of the T'ondrakec'is found considerable support among the people; this movement which spread over the entire country, causing serious disturbances for almost two centuries, was in some measure a popular uprising of the peasantry and the poorer classes of the towns against the feudal lords and the wealthy hierarchy of the church.[57]

Basing themselves on Engels' interpretation of the German peasant movement of the sixteenth century, Soviet Armenian scholars see the Paulician and T'ondrakec'i sectarians as a proletarian social movement in revolt against the oppression of a feudal society.[58] Under the influence of Weber and Troeltsch a good many recent writers have also explained medieval heresy in terms of economic, social and political movements.

There is a connection between sectarian revolts and the rise of commercial activity, the rise of the cities, and the extension of monetary and economic relations in general and therefore a thesis of materialist motivation is valid.[59] Some recent studies have dissociated Paulicianism and T'ondrakianism from any substratum of social and economic protest. This is for the most part to be attributed to a disregard of the proper historical method of study of problems of time and place, and it is indispensable to determine with precision the historical period and context of the T'ondrakec'i movements.

With this historical background in mind, I shall attempt to show the interrelation of constituent social, religious, economic and political factors behind the T'ondrakec'i movement.

CHAPTER IV

THE ORIGIN OF THE T'ONDRAKEC'I MOVEMENT: SMBAT ZAREHAWAN AND HIS CONTEMPORARIES

This sect took its name from the village of T'ondrak situated in the canton of Apahunik' at the foot of mount Aladag.[1] The founder of the sect, Smbat, from the village of Zarehawan, which lay further east in the Armenian district of Całkotn, had migrated to T'ondrak and from there spread his heresy.[2]

The indecisive evidence of the sources with regard to the chronology of the sect has led to a good deal of speculation. Many scholars consider it to have originated in the first half of the ninth century, others in the second half, and some in the early tenth century.

Asołik, writing a century later about the election of kat'ołikos Yovhannēs Drasxanakertc'i V which took place in 898, states:

> After him in the year 346 of our era [16th April 887 - 17th April 898] the patriarchal throne was occupied by the Lord Yovhannēs of Dvin, the orator and historian who held it for twenty-two years. It was under his pontificate that Smbat, the leader of the T'ondrakec'is the enemy of all institutions, made his appearance. He came from the village of Zarehawan, in the district of Całkotn.[3]

Grigor Magistros states that the beginning of the sect is to be dated 170 years before his own time, that is to say, in the first half of the ninth century, of Smbat he writes: "This accursed one appeared in the days of the Lord Yovhannēs and Smbat Bagratuni".[4] Most scholars have been under the impression that Grigor Magistros was quoting Asołik. But this impression is proved to be false when we consider Grigor's other information about the T'ondrakec'is:

> For 170 years, thirteen patriarchs of Great Armenia, and as many of Ałwank' and numerous bishops and innumerable priests and deacons admonished you and you did not hear. They spoke and confuted you, but you were not ashamed. They anathematized and proscribed you, and you have not repented.[5]

In another of his letters, Grigor states that the "T'ondrakec'is" for more than 200 years infested the whole land, and raised up the fire-altar of their lust and lewdness". In the same letter Grigor writes: "prior to ourselves, many generals and magistrates have given them over to the sword" and by his time fifteen Armenian kat'ołikoses had anathematized them.[6]

At first sight it may appear that in Grigor's accounts there are contradictions. If we bear in mind the fact that Grigor wrote these letters in A.D. 1050, it would suggest that on one occasion he puts the date for the beginning of the sect around 870-880 and on another occasion around 840-850. But in actual fact there is no discrepancy. When Grigor wrote that the sect had existed for more than two hundred years and that it had been condemned by fifteen patriarchs, he had in mind the very early days of the movement. While his 170 years of campaign against the sectarians refers to the period of active and organised persecution. So the date of the origin of the sect, or the date of Smbat Zarehawan's operations, Grigor puts in the first part of the ninth century, during the kat'ołikosate of Yovhannēs IV of Ovayak' (833-855) and *sparapet* (generalissimo) Smbat Bagratuni (822-855) – also called Smbat the Confessor or Smbat Abū'l-'Abbās. That Grigor's "In the days of Lord Yovhannēs" is a reference not to Yovhannēs Drasxanakertc'i the historian (897-931), but to Yovhannēs of Ovayak' is borne out by the facts. Petros Getadarj (1019-1036, 1038-1054) the kat'ołikos contemporary with Grigor Magistros (990-1058) was indeed the thirteenth patriarch after Yovhannēs of Ovayak', whilst Yovhannēs V would be not the fifteenth but the ninth.[7] It would appear that both Grigor Magistros and Asołik got their information about the inception of the sect and the appearance of Smbat Zarehawan from the *Treatise against the T'ondrakec'is* by Anania of Narek, which unfortunately is no longer in existence. So that according to Anania the origin of the sect must have been assigned to the period of kat'ołikos Yovhannēs and Smbat Bagratuni which Grigor Magistros has interpreted correctly – while Asołik had incorrectly identified Yovhannēs IV Ovayak' with Yovhannēs V the historian, and Smbat Bagratuni with Smbat *Nahatak* (Smbat the Martyr, 890-914). The coincidence of the Smbats and two Yovhannēs's easily explains the confusion, especially since Armenian chroniclers often failed to distinguish the *sparapet* Smbat from his grandson, king Smbat the Martyr.

There is further evidence to support this conclusion in the *History* of Mxitar Ayrivanec'i who confirms under A.D. 821 that "Smbat called Abū'l-'Abbās, [was] a member of the T'ondrakec'is".[8] When speaking of Smbat the Curopalate, Mxit'ar adds that in A.D. 822 "from his namesake, his grandson [Smbat Curopalate] emerged the sect of the T'ondrakec'is during the days of kat'ołikos David II Kakałec'i" (806-833).[9] In the work of Ayrivanec'i the grandson of Curopalate Smbat Abū'l-'Abbās is presented as a Chalcedonian opponent of Step'annos Siwnec'i. The fact that Armenian chroniclers represent Chalcedonianism as just another schism or sect, led Mxit'ar Ayrivanec'i to confuse Smbat Abū'l-'Abbās the Chalcedonian with Smbat Zarehawan. I shall return to this false identification again, but at this point what is significant is that Mxit'ar Ayrivanec'i also regards Smbat Bagratuni, the kat'ołikos David II Kakałec'i,

Yovhannēs IV Ovayak', and the founder of the sect of the T'ondrakec'is, as contemporaries in the period 822-855.

Lastly, the date for the beginning of the T'ondrakec'i movement or the appearance of Smbat of Zarehawan can be established beyond doubt on the basis of further important evidence. This is found in a letter by Grigor of Narek written to the heretical abbot of the monastery of Kčaw, which we find preserved in the *Book of Letters.*[10]

Grigor of Narek in his *Letters to the abbot of Kčaw*, when writing about the persecution of the T'ondrakec'is, honours the Saracen emir Aplvard (Abū'l-ward) in the following manner, "to mix your blood with the blood of those who were massacred by the sword of that avenging infidel, the emir Aplvard, who proved himself indeed a rod of anger in the hand of the Lord Jesus". He then adds that the same emir had killed the ancestors of the T'ondrakec'is, "a valiant man who destroyed and put to an infamous death their accursed ancestors". In the killing of the T'ondrakec'is' leader, Smbat Zarehawanc'i, the emir had also said, "If Christ arose on the third day, then since you call yourself 'Christ' I will slay you and bury you and if you shall come to life again after thirty, then I will know that you are Christ". Grigor considers both Zarehawanc'i and Abū'l-Ward as heretics "for he was close to them and to their bitter madness" because both were enemies of the Armenian Church.[11]

The identity of this Saracen emir has led to a good deal of discussion. Conybeare does not identify him[12], Markwart read 'Abd al-Barr rather than Abū'l-Ward (Apelbard).[13] In the Byzantine epic *Digenes Akrites*, among the numerous personages involved, there is also mention of a certain emir 'Απλορραβδις of Mayyāfāriḳīn:"My own country is Mayyāfāriḳīn, you have heard of Haplorrabdis the emir of all, he is my father, my mother is Melanthia".[14]

The Greek historian P. Karolides[15] identified 'Απλορραβδις with the emir of Mayyāfāriḳīn 'Abd al-Raḥīm ('Αβδουραχιμ); J. Mavrogordato[16] suggests that 'Απλορραβδις is 'Αποταγλε (Abū-Taghlib) of the seventies of the tenth century who allied himself with Bardas Skleros in 976.

Rejecting B. Sargisean's[17] mistaken hypothesis the "Aplvard" mentioned by Narekac'i might be identified with either Abu'l-Haydja or Abū-Dulaf (Apu Tlup') who both lived in the tenth century, A. Hovhannisyan[18] correctly deduced that he was to be identified with the first Ḳaysite emir, Abū'l-Ward himself. However, he further concluded that Smbat Zarehawanc'i had appeared in the first half of the ninth century and moved the beginning of Abū'l-Ward's rule to the 830's. As we have already seen, this Ḳaysite emir belongs in the sixties of the same century. He ruled Apahunik', with the city of Manazkert, and became a lord of considerable power "a valiant man" only thereafter. It is therefore incorrect to put him on the eve of Bugha's expedition, at a time when the Djaḥḥāfid Sawāda himself was still alive.

In his discussion of the same problem, S. Połosyan[19] shifts the other Abu'l-Ward who lived in the tenth century, to the beginning of that century thus completely ignoring the existence of other Ḳaysites who intervened between the two Abū'l-Wards. According to him, the name of the first Ḳaysite emir who lived in the ninth century was Aplbaṙ, whereas the last Ḳaysite living in the tenth century was called Abi-l-Vard. In Arabic, the form *Abi-* is the genitive case of *Abū-i*, "father", and the name of both Ḳaysite emirs was in fact Abū'l-Ward.[20]

We should also note that the founder of the T'ondrakec'i sect, Smbat of Zarehawan, was born in the village of Zarehawan located in the district of Całkotn in the region of Ayrarat, but that he found refuge in the lands of the Ḳaysite emirs at the village of T'ondrak in the province of Apahunik'. The district of Całkotn, which was part of the Bagratid domain, was evidently not a safe place for heretical activities directed against the Armenian Church, whereas under the dominion of the Muslim emir, Smbat could feel relatively safe from the attacks of his opponents. From the testimony of Grigor of Narek, however, we see that the refuge in Apahunik' was to prove costly for the founder of the new sect. If in truly Armenian provinces the target of the sectarian struggle was the feudal aristocracy, so that the movement bore an essentially social stamp, then in the domains of the Ḳaysites, this class struggle was inextricably bound with liberation movements directed against the foreign conquerors. The rule of the Ḳaysite Abū'l-Ward was doubly burdensome for the population of Apahunik' in that he was not only an exploiter but a foreign conqueror as well. It is consequently no accident that he should have drowned the movement of Smbat of Zarehawan in blood. We observe the same characteristics among the Paulicians, who in purely Byzantine territory fought exclusively against the ruling class, whereas in border districts their movement took on a certain colouration of anti-Arab drive for liberation. When the T'ondrakian movement subsequently acquired greater momentum in the tenth century we know that Arab emirates of Armenia once again provided the setting for its activity.[22]

The identity of Smbat has also aroused a great deal of speculation. Conybeare makes the suggestion that the heresiarch Smbat and the *sparapet* Smbat Bagratuni were actually the same person, and that heresy was rife in the Bagratuni house.[23] This identification seems very doubtful. It is true that both Samuēl of Ani and Mxit'ar Ayrivanec'i attribute the foundation of the T'ondrakec'i sect to Smbat called Abū'l-'Abbās the son of Ašot and date this 824.[24] This is a reference to the *sparapet* Smbat, the son of Ašot Msaker, who received the name of Abū'l-'Abbās during his stay as a hostage at the court of the Caliph al-Ma'mūn.[25] These two references are late. Furthermore the feud, presumably on religious grounds, between the kat'ołikos Yovhannēs V and the *sparapet* Smbat, postulated by Conybeare, cannot be substantiated. The dispute was between the kat'ołikos and Smbat's elder brother, Bagarat Bagratuni. It is also known that when Bagarat succeeded in having Yovhannēs of Ovayak' replaced by a kat'ołikos of his own choosing, Smbat called a synod which in opposition to Bagarat set Yovhannēs of Ovayak' once more on the pontifical throne.[26] Finally, the accusation of sodomy which the historian T'ovma Arcruni lays against the Bagratuni dynasty, and in which Conybeare sees a hidden reference to heresy, cannot be taken very seriously. T'ovma, the official historian of the Arcruni court, the rivals of the Bagratids, takes every opportunity to blacken the reputation of the ruling house.[27]

Two more attempts at identifying Smbat of Zarehawan have been made. Conybeare suggests the possibility that he was that Smbat Bagratuni who was known as "Xosrov Šnum". This is based on the information given by Grigor Magistros that Smbat of Zarehawan had learned his doctrine from a Persian physician.[28] We know that Smbat "Xosrov Šnum" lived during the patriarchate of Yovhannēs III of Bagaran (590-611). Step'annos Ōrbelean accuses yet another Smbat Bagratuni, *sparapet* in 691, of being a diophysite and an enemy of the orthodox clergy.[29] These identifications, which completely disagree with the precise chronology of Grigor Magistros, seem altogether implausible, especially since no Smbat is known to Vrt'anēs K'ert'oł or to Yovhannēs Ōjnec'i, who would hardly have ignored such an important heresiarch had he lived in a period preceding or contemporary with their own.

About Smbat of Zarehawan there is very little in the sources. Under such circumstances we can only form our opinion of Smbat of Zarehawan's teachings and operations from the writings about him by his adversaries. The authors of such apologetics are very evasive and their information about the teachings and ideology strictly censored. This impression is well supported by a confession of Aristakēs Lastiverc'i, who devotes two chapters to the T'ondrakec'is. He writes: "But as for their filthy observances, we deemed it indecent to commit them to writing, for they are too loathsome, and since it is not everyone that is proof against what he hears, the writing down of the many sins might draw listeners into lust, or even lead them to commit such things themselves."[30] What these doctrines were, will be discussed in due course; but at this stage we will consider the possible sources of Smbat of Zarehawan's ideology, which may help to put the whole movement into its right historical context and perspective.

Grigor Magistros writes that Smbat was trying to assimilate all sectarian movements of his time and before him into a single ideological unit: "This sect drew not on two or three sources only, but embraced all that was ever heretical – soothsaying, palmistry, incantations and magical arts, infidelities, wicked poisons, all in the single brew of their heresy, when they consented to that enemy of God, that hedgebreaker, diabolical madman, Smbat, giving them their laws . . . ".[31] Grigor defines the sect as "the sum of all evil that can possibly in this life come into a man's head".[32]

In studies of the T'ondrakec'i movement, it has hitherto been viewed and presented as an extension of ancient sectarian movements (Manichaeans, Messalians, Borborites and Paulicians)[33], on the basis of similarity of ideas, without troubling to show how this was accomplished. This is possible when ideas are interpreted in terms of other ideas, as if history took place in an intellectual test-tube. But, it is not sufficient to study the affiliation of one group to another on the basis of similarity of doctrine alone; it is also essential to see the affiliation in the context of each movement's concrete historical situation and surroundings.

In this respect no comprehensive study has been made of the non-Christian movements in the neighbouring countries of Armenia at the time, and their possible affiliation with the T'ondrakec'is of Armenia.[34] This deficiency is due to the fact that the sources available are scanty and that until now the chronology of the origin of the T'ondrakec'is was not accurate. Not enough attention is given to the significant fact that the T'ondrakec'i movement originated at a time when in neighbouring countries, in Iran and Byzantium under the leadership of the Khurramites (Joyful Ones) and the Paulicians, socio-religious revolts were taking place, about which Smbat of Zarehawan could not have been unaware. The T'ondrakec'i sect similarly found considerable support among the people; it spread over the entire country causing serious disturbances for almost two centuries, and was in some measure also a popular uprising of the peasantry and the poorer classes of the cities and towns against the feudal lords and the wealthy hierarchy of the church.

There is support in the sources for the supposition that the T'ondrakec'is, the Khurramites, and the Paulicians and the many affiliations between them on the basis of doctrine and ideology are to be explained not on the basis of direct succession or continuity, but by the politico-socio-economic conditions which gave rise to similar movements, creating in some cases not only internal ideological affiliation but also external relationship. The attack of the emir Aplvard I on Smbat was not an isolated incident, it had more than a local significance.

In 746, a rebellion broke out in Khurāsān. At this period an extraordinary heresiarch of Iranian origin, Abū Muslim, appeared in Khurāsān with the mission of directing the movement of insurrection in that province. In a short time the rebels under Abū Muslim, profiting from the internal discords in the Umayyad army and the continuing political discontent prevailing in that province, forced the Umayyad governor to leave. In 750 Marwān II, caliph since 745, was defeated and the Umayyad dynasty came to an end. Abū Muslim "in his religious propaganda seems to have amalgamated the doctrines of Islam with ancient popular beliefs, particularly with that of metempsychosis, and to have pretended to be an incarnation of the divinity."[35]

Another scholar is of the opinion that "We do not clearly know what promises or teachings Abū Muslim gave to bring the masses over, but we may assert with some probability that the idea of the incarnation of God in Muḥammad, in Alī and his descendants, or finally in Abū Muslim himself, played the leading role."[36] Whatever the role of Abū Muslim in the 'Abbāsid revolt, his position was not very comfortable in the new dynasty. His relationship with the new dynasty, which owed its success largely to him, became increasingly uncomfortable. His great prestige and power was enough to alarm the 'Abbāsids. The accession of al-Manṣūr in 753-754 marked the beginning of the crisis. Abū Muslim was treacherously killed. His memory remained and some even denied that he was dead and foretold his return to "spread justice in the world".[37] On this foundation several sects arose. In Khurāsān, around 776, a man appeared who became known as al-Muqanna' (Veiled Prophet), since he wore a veil to hide his countenance, which for his followers would have been sinister to behold because of its "shining light". His claim was that he should be looked upon as the incarnation of prophethood and fulfiller of the work of the murdered Abū Muslim. He gathered a large body of supporters, who were openly dissatisfied with the 'Abbāsid policy, and only after a very long struggle was he defeated.

From the remnants of his followers, from surviving advocates of the Mazdakism of Sasanian times and from economic malcontents, another sect was formed in Ādharbāydjān in 816-817 under the leadership of Bābak, the Arabic form of the Iranian Papak.

He was noticed by Djawidan ibn Sahl, after whose death Bābak claimed that the spirit of the previous leader had entered into him, and he began to stir up the people living in the region of al-Badhdh, situated in the region of Arrān,[38] not far from the Araxes.

It is insufficiently realised that the so-called Persian renaissance in Khurāsān had a momentous sequel in Armenia. By the beginning of the tenth century a great Iranian movement came from the Caspian provinces. At the head of the hosts of Gitan and Daylam a new set of rulers ousted the Arabs from their last positions held in Iran, and round this new power a fringe of other small principalities was created. Even then the Arabs adopted a system of indirect control of Armenia through the agency of the Bagratid princes (806-1045), and this policy was conditioned by the direction of the imperial and commercial roads passing through Dvin and Ardabīl, which played an important role. Even during the period of wars between the Muslims and the Byzantines, which hampered direct exchanges between the two parties, the Bagratid kingdom became an intermediary in the communications between Iraq and the Black Sea. When Sādj Afshīn addressed reproaches to Smbat (890-913) about the duplicity of his relations with the Byzantine empire, the Armenian king drew his attention to the material advantages which accrued to the Arabs from this attitude.[39] But to the east of this autonomous area the Arabs retained the system of direct rule in Ādharbāydjān.

The Muslim sources hint only indirectly at the facts of this "most dangerous movement"[40], which Movsēs Dasxuranc'i has recorded in great detail and which throw a lurid light on Bābak's activities.[41] He imparted new vigour to this religious and social movement which distinguished itself by its long duration (816-837), leadership and cohesion. His following was drawn mainly from the peasantry,[42] whose support he won by preaching and practising the break-up of large estates and the distribution of land. The principles they advocated were socialist, while they were also relatively tolerant as regards religion.

We may safely assume that in these movements there were national and social undercurrents. According to Abū-Muḥammad:

> The reason why most of these sects deserted the religion of Islam is basically this. The Persians originally were the masters of a large kingdom and had the upper hand over all the nations. They were in consequence possessed of such mighty self-esteem that they called themselves "nobles" and "sons", while the rest of mankind were regarded by them as slaves. But when they were visited [by God] and their empire taken away from them by the Arabs – the same Arabs who in the estimation of the Persians, possessed the least dignity of all nations – the matter weighed much more heavily upon them, and the calamity assumed double proportions in their eyes and they decided to beguile Islam. Among their rebels were Sunbad, al-Muqanna, Bābak and others.[43]

A review of the conflict that Arab historians record in the years A.H. 201-220 (A.D. 816/7-835) supports this suggestion. Ṭabarī lists a series of generals appointed by the caliph al-Ma'mūn to fight Bābak and an equal number of defeats. "In the year 204 Yaḥyā b. Mu'adh was set against Bābak – in 205 al-Ma'mūn appointed 'Isā b. Muḥammad – then in 207 he appointed 'Abdullah b. Ṭāhir – and later 'Alī b. Hishām", so the record goes.[44]

About that time the Arab emir Sawāda ('Abd al-Ḥamīd al-Djaḥḥāfī) raided Siwnik', and the local prince, Vasak, appealed for help to the famous rebel and heresiarch Bābak (in Armenian *Baban*). The rebel responded to this call and married Vasak's daughter. But Bābak committed excesses in the region of Lake Sevan (A.D. 828) where he destroyed the famous convent of Makenoc'. Movsēs Dasxuranc'i writes – "The next year Baban [Bābak] passed into the canton of Gełark'uni and put about 15,000 inhabitants to the sword, and burned the great monastery of Makenoc'".[45] According to Movsēs "another ruler Sahl (son of Sunbat) revolted in Arrān during the Caliphate of al-Mu'taṣim (218-227/833-842), and it appears that for a short time the interests of Sahl and Bābak coincided."[46] The Khurramites also seem to have had a working alliance with the Byzantine emperor against the common foe.

After a long struggle, Bābak was compelled to abandon his mountain fortress and flee with his brother Abdullah in A.D. 837. Bābak tried to escape to the protection of the emperor Theophilus, then engaged in a bitter struggle with the Muslim forces around Tarsus. He sent a message to Sahl b. Sunbat and the latter came out to meet him. Ṭabarī's report on Bābak's flight records that on meeting him Sahl recognized him, kissed his hand and said, "O lord there is no one worthier to receive you than myself. You know my place. I have nothing to do with the government [the sultan]. You know what has happened to me and you know my country. All the *bat'riqs*[47] who are here are related to you, and children have been borne to you from their [houses]."[48] All this suggests that Sahl had personal relations with Bābak.[49]

Although Sahl had been an ally of Bābak, he was prevailed upon by Afshīn to surrender Bābak. Movsēs Dasxuranc'i writes: "In the same year the Lord Sahl Smbatean[50] [Sahl b. Sunbat] captured the rebel Baban [Bābak], the murderous, world-ravaging, blood-thirsty beast, and delivered him into the hands of the emir Momnin [al-Ma'mūn]".[51] For this service Sahl received, according to al-Mas'ūdi,[52] a royal robe, a crown, and a horse, and was exempted from tribute, all of which amounted to an official investiture as ruler of Albania.[53] Movsēs Dasxuranc'i confirms this fact with the obvious exaggeration that Sahl "obtained sovereignty over Armenia, Georgia and Albania, to rule authoritatively and royally over all."[54] All this suggests that the Caliphate honoured Sahl's signal service highly and forgave him all his previous misdeeds.

In 840, Afshīn, the conqueror of Bābak, was put to death on the charge of alleged Magian (Manichaean?) leanings, and of assuming privileges traditionally belonging to a ruler. The execution of Bābak did not put an end to the Khurramite movement.

There remained a number of important problems, political, social and national, between the Arab conquerors and the local populations, particularly the Armenians. It is significant that the messianic concept of a mahdi[55] and the occurrence of the above events either coincide or are contemporary with the beginning of the T'ondrakec'is and the appearance of Smbat of Zarehawan. There are two very important references which confirm direct association of the T'ondrakec'is with the above events.

As discussed above, the Ḳaysite emir Aplvard I persecuted Smbat of Zarehawan and his supporters around 830-840. Grigor of Narek honours this service rendered by the Muslim emir very highly. Grigor calls him "a certain valiant man", "a rod of wrath in the hand of Christ" and "sword of the avenging infidel".[56] According to Grigor, Aplvard I executed the self-styled Iamres[57] saying: "Since you call yourself Christ, and Christ rose on the third day, I will slay you and bury you, and if you rise even after thirty days I will know that you are Christ".[58] Grigor of Narek likewise says that "they dared to call the head of their abominable sect a Christ".[59] In the same letter Grigor writes "the foul Smbat, a second Simon, allowed himself to be worshipped by his disciples".[60] In the twelfth century Paul of Tarōn condemned the T'ondrakec'is who "say that Christ is a mere man".[61]

According to Grigor, Smbat was killed by the Muslim emir because of his claim to be "Christ". The T'ondrakec'i movement in Armenia was not just a revolt seeking innovations within the Armenian church. If it had confined itself only to religious reforms without drawing from them socio-economic and national conclusions, there would be no reason for the alarm and the subsequent persecution which its adherents suffered. It seems that they did draw the inevitable conclusions and began a bitter struggle against the feudal aristocracy, the apparent injustices and the oppression of the lower classes, winning the support of the peasant population. It was this dimension of the movement which compelled the civil and religious authorities, including the "infidel" overlords, to persecute them. The execution of Smbat by the emir Aplvard I cannot be understood and interpreted in any other way.

Hovhannisyan[62] interprets the fact the Smbat of Zarehawan called himself "Christ" as an indication that he received these tenets from the Muslim sect with whom he had connections. This theory cannot be maintained because this messianic concept expressed in the titles "Saviour", "Christ", "Prophet", "Paraclete", "Mahdi" is a feature common to all eastern sects and its origins are to be sought in Gnosticism, and, therefore, there is no reason to suppose that one sect learnt it from the other. It is not a characteristic of any sect as such. At the basis of many ancient religions there is the firm conviction that in the end a "Saviour" will appear, who will liberate the world from the bondage of evil, will put an end to all injustices, and establish equality among all men. It was this very belief among the masses which the heresiarchs took advantage of when they claimed to be "Saviour", "Christ", "Mahdi", "Perfect prophet". Thus any exchange of ideas between the various sects, would strengthen and stabilise certain already existing concepts.

The second important testimony is found in a letter of Grigor Magistros. He states that Smbat the heresiarch had learned his evil erroneous teaching from a Persian physician and astrologer whom they called *Mǰusik*[63]. Unfortunately, the identity of the physician in question is not known. According to Ališan,[64] *Mǰusik* is the transcription of the Persian word for "*Magus*" and has the same meaning. In the writings of the fifteenth century chronicler Mxit'ar Aparanc'i, we find the name *Mǰusik* in the form of *Mrǰusik* which according to Ačaṙyan[65] is derived from the Armenian name *Mrǰunik*. On the basis of the latter suggestion Hovhannisyan concludes that Smbat's teacher was not a Persian but an Armenian affiliated with the Persian Magis and thus rejects the thesis that Smbat's ideas came from Persia. According to the testimony of Mxit'ar Aparanc'i and Grigor Magistros[66] all the teachers of Smbat, (Mǰusik, T'odoros, Ananē, Cyril, Joseph, Yesu, Sargis, Ark'a) were Armenian sectarians. On the other hand, in view of the doctrinal similarity and the possibility of geographical and historical contact, there seems to be no reason to completely exclude the possibility of outside influence.

CHAPTER V

THE RELATION OF THE T'ONDRAKEC'I MOVEMENT WITH THE PAULICIANS

The relation of the Paulicians to the T'ondrakec'is has been generally accepted.[1] Like Conybeare, Garsoian sees "a striking similarity of doctrine and practice between the sects"[2] and she is convinced that we can speak of a certain continuity between the two sects – the Paulician and the T'ondrakec'i. "The identity of the two heresies, however, is evident not only from the similarity of their doctrines, but also from the specific identification of the T'ondrakec'is as Paulicians made in the eleventh century by Grigor Magistros."[3] As a result, Garsoian tends to shift from the terminology of the source to the term "Paulician". Thus she speaks of Prince Vrveṙ of Širi being accused of Paulicianism[4] rather than of being a T'ondrakec'i as the sources state.[5] Garsoian's approach is not entirely justifiable because it is based on the assumption that the book *The Key of Truth* is an authentic T'ondrakec'i text. There is little doubt that *The Key of Truth* was used by sectarians with beliefs most probably derived from the Paulicians, but we cannot be sure that their beliefs had not evolved considerably since the Middle Ages and that *The Key of Truth* was not a presentation of evolving views as they stood in 1782. Garsoian, who persuasively argues that Paulician views underwent a variety of changes in Byzantium, should be equally willing to accept that Armenian doctrine was not static either. For this reason, I find the arguments for accepting *The Key of Truth* as a Paulician or T'ondrakec'i text to be insufficiently proved. I shall give the objections to this assumption in a separate chapter.

The relation of the T'ondrakec'is to the Paulicians is also noted by many Armenian scholars on very different grounds. Hovhannisyan, Yuzbašyan and Mnac'akanyan[6] suggest that the two movements should be associated, not only on the basis of similarity of doctrine, but more significantly because both were national movements, seeking socio-economic and political reforms.

According to Garsoian, the two kat'ołikoses nearest to the epoch of Grigor Magistros, Yovhannēs Drasxanakertc'i the historian (899-931) and Yovhannēs IV of Ovayak (833-855), did not concern themselves with the heretics; on the other hand, Yovhannēs

Ōjnec'i was renowned for his attacks on heretics and on Paulicians in particular.[7] Her second argument for making this identification is that the "punishment decreed for the heretics condemned at the Council of Šahapivan (447), who are probably Paulicians"[8], namely the branding of the heretic on the forehead with the sign of a fox, is the specific punishment used against the T'ondrakec'is, "it is mentioned as such by both Aristakēs Lastiverc'i and Grigor Magistros".[9]

Both these arguments seem insufficiently proved and their very weakness lies in the fact that they are based on two suppositions. One, that the heresy referred to in Canon XIV and XIX of the Council of Šahapivan is a "reference to the Paulicians in Armenia"; the difficulty of accepting this thesis is enormous. Second, it is dangerous to draw the conclusion that the punishment decreed against the heretics justifies this identification. The form of punishment, namely the branding of the heretic on the forehead with the sign of a fox, is not a specific punishment for either the Paulicians nor the T'ondrakec'is. It is widely used for all heretics.

The letters of Grigor Magistros are our chief Armenian source for T'ondrakec'i history and doctrine. When speaking about the T'ondrakec'is, Grigor Magistros constantly identifies them with the Manichaeans. Thus one of his letters written against the T'ondrakec'is is entitled *Answer to the letter of the T'ulaili, who were a remnant of the new Manichaeans [T'ondrakec'eac'n]*.[10] While in the 69th letter the author writes directly "who were taught by the Manichaeans and named *T'ondrakec'ik'*."[11]

In another passage from his letter to the Syrian Kat'ołikos, Grigor writes "But others [are taught] after the manner of the Manichaeans".[12] Which heretics are referred to by the name of "Manichaeans"? In my view Grigor Magistros was referring to the Paulicians. During the centuries after the rise and disappearance of the Manichaeans, when Manichaeism became no longer identifiable as a sect, the Paulicians in particular were constantly referred to as Manichaeans. Thus Peter of Sicily's *History*, which is an important source of information for Paulician history, is entitled *Ιστορία χρειώδης ἔλεγχός τε καὶ ἀνατροπὴ τῆς κενῆς καὶ ματαίας αἱρέσεως τῶν Μανιχαίων, τῶν καὶ Παυλικιάνων λεγομένων, προσωποποιηθεῖσα ὡς πρὸς τὸν ἀρχιεπίσκοπον Βουλγαρίας*.[13]

The author insists that the Paulicians are the same as the Manichaeans *Οὐ γὰρ ἄλλοι οὗτοι καὶ ἄλλοι ἐκεῖνοι, ἀλλ' οἱ αὐτοὶ Παυλικιάνοι καὶ Μανιχαῖοι ὑπάρχουσιν*.[14]

His first work on the Paulicians, Photius or pseudo-Photius has entitled *Διήγησις περι τῆς Μανιχαίων ἀναβλαστήσεως*.[15] The chapter on the Paulicians included in the *Chronicle* of George the Monk, refers to the Paulicians as Manichaeans.[16] This interchange of terms is not accidental.

One of the characteristic features of Paulician doctrine is its dualism. They distinguished between the Heavenly Father, who has no power in this world but will be Lord of the Future, and the other God, the Creator of the world, who holds all the power in the visible world.[17] The Greek authorities insisted that all recanting Paulicians be forced to recite the Creed, confessing the Trinity and the one true God, creator of heaven and earth, and that they be closely questioned to make certain that they interpreted these beliefs in Orthodox fashion. It was the dualistic doctrine which gave reason for Greek apologists to see affinities between the Paulicians and the Manichaeans. Byzantium was well acquainted with the Manichaeans and the term was extensively employed as a term of abuse, like the term *mcłnē* (filthiness) in medieval Armenian literature.

However, at this point it must be noted that this alleged relationship between the Manichaeans and the Paulicians is a smear. This identification of the Paulicians with the Manichaeans was the principal weapon of the Orthodox writers for their campaign against the Paulicians.

Now the Paulicians were defined as Manichaeans not only in Byzantium but also in Armenia. Thus Grigor of Narek entitles one of his chapters in his *Book of Lamentations*, "Discourse concerning the church against the Manichaeans who are Paulicians".[18] This sub-title is to be found in one of the oldest and best manuscripts, copied at the request of Nersēs Lambronac'i in A.D. 1173.[19] It is also interesting to note that in certain manuscripts, the name T'ondrakec'i is substituted for Paulicians. The sub-title in one of the editions of the *Book of Lamentations* is "Discourse concerning the church against the foul T'ondrakec'i sect, new Manichaeans".[20]

There seems to be no doubt that when Grigor Magistros uses the name T'ondrakec'i in conjunction with the Manichaeans, as he constantly does, he has in mind the Paulicians. It is true that in one place he writes: "but others [are taught] after the manner of the Manichaeans, whom they anathematize at the same time, as they pursue the same practices".[21] But nowhere in the works of Grigor Magistros do we find evidence that the T'ondrakec'is "anathematize" the Paulicians. This gives us reason to believe that in that passage the author is referring to the actual Manichaeans. This is well supported, in that all apologists who have written about the Paulicians without exception accepted that the Paulicians "anathematize" Mani and his disciple, Paul of Samosata and his brother John.

In his letter to the kat'ołikos of Syria, speaking of the T'ondrakec'is of whom he had first-hand information, he characterises them as follows: "Here you see the Paulicians who got their poison from Paul of Samosata".[22] This is a reference to Paul of Samosata the semi-legendary founder of the sect, from whom it is supposed to have taken its name. Thereafter, Grigor describes very briefly some of the teachings and tenets of the Paulicians which do not in any way contradict the information given by the Greek sources. According to Grigor Magistros, the Paulicians call themselves "Christians".[23] Peter of Sicily and Petrus Higumenus are also of the opinion that the name "Paulicians" was given to the sectarians by their opponents, since they called themselves "Christians".[24]

So the two passages from Grigor Magistros' letters show that the author saw no distinction between the Paulicians of the eleventh century and the T'ondrakec'is. This is also not just a coincidence. This view has been expressed in the title of the 67th letter from which we have taken most of our quotations. The title is: *The answer to the letter of the kat'ołikos of the Syrians, at the time when he was dux in Vaspurakan and Tarōn. After the Manichaeans had been rooted out of the territory of the Greeks and from T'ondrak, the remnant of this condemned race went to the kat'ołikos of the Syrians in the city of Amid, to try to win him over by their deceit.*[25] According to Grigor, the Byzantine Paulicians were "Manichaeans from the land of the Greeks" and the Armenian T'ondrakec'is were "Manichaeans from T'ondra", in short the followers of the same movement. Grigor Magistros carried out an active persecution of the T'ondrakec'is within his province.[26] And those remnants which tried to take refuge in Amid were not successful, for Grigor warned the kat'ołikos about the danger of accepting the sectarians and advised him "not to have mercy on them or have any communication with them or deign to look on them" but instead encouraged the kat'ołikos to "curse them whenever they come into thy mind".[27] This identification of the Paulicians with the Manichaeans is a feature of the Byzantine sources of which Grigor Magistros was well informed. That this was so can be proved by examining a single fact.

In "*Šnavank'* there lived men clad as monks and a multitude of whorish women so we ordered their residences to be pulled down and burned and their tenants to be driven out of our territories".[28] This is a reference to certain refugees who had settled in a place called *Šnavank'* which Yuzbašyan and Ter-Mkrttschian[29] translate as "the community of dogs", rather than "the dog monastery" and take it to be a reference to *τοὺς κατοικοῦντας* Κύνας *τὴν τοῦ* Κύνος *χώραν*.[30]

Petrus Higumenus recalls that the Paulicians of the "Koloneia" community were called Κοινοχωρῖτας, while Peter of Sicily, instead of *κοινοχωρῖτας*, used another word *κυνοχωρῖτας*, which means "the community of dogs". He insists that the heretics are "dogs" and live in *κυνοχωρῖτας*.[32]

According to Yuzbašyan, the Pau[illegible]ement was a peasant revolt. Its driving force was the community which oppose[illegible] ruling minority. They were trying to re-establish the traditional Christian "Communal" life. And so the term *κοινοχωρῖτας* is most appropriate in the present context. But in medieval Greek the "*οι*" diphthong and the letter "*υ*" have the same sound. So Peter of Sicily gives the original word an offensive meaning by replacing *κοινοχωρῖτας* by *κυνοχωρῖτας*. As a result the pronunciation of the two forms would have been indistinguishable,[33] but the two words have quite distinct meanings. We have thus indicated that Grigor Magistros was closely acquainted with the Byzantine sources. Grigor names with unmistakable offensive intention *Šnavank'*, the Armenian translation of *κυνοχωρῖτας*[34], the location where the Paulician refugees came to settle after the fall of Tephrike in 872.

Grigor Magistros' presentation of the history of the T'ondrakec'i movement as identical with the Paulician movement is not entirely arbitrary. We will now investigate the process by which such affinities could have occurred.

The historical contact between the two movements is beyond doubt, as is the favour shown to the Paulicians by the Isaurian emperors. We now know from the detailed studies of Kaegi and Bart'ikyan that the main support for Constantine V's iconoclastic programme came not so much from the thematic armies, whose allegiances were erratic, as from the specially recruited and indoctrinated *tagmata* stationed in the capital. These were the soldiers who were to disrupt the Iconodule council at the church of the Holy Apostles, and who would have to be decoyed out of the capital and dismissed by the empress Irene before the summoning of the second council of Nicaea. In this connection, a remark in the patriarch Nikephoros' *Refutatio et eversio* is particularly interesting. The patriarch says that Constantine V "had indoctrinated the *tagmata* against the Orthodox, and particularly those detachments which he had recruited for the capital from the herdsmen". The *Vita S. Stephani Junioris*[35] reveals Constantine's attempts to control the religious beliefs and practices of his troops, since it makes a special point of the fact that as a result of the upheavals among the members of the Paulician community, one of their leaders, a certain Joseph, moved to the vicinity of Pisidian Antioch in the first half of the eighth century. Is it beyond the realms of possibility that some of the herdsmen enrolled for the Emperor's loyal and belligerently iconoclastic *tagmata* were Joseph's Paulician followers? Be that as it may, Nikephoros says explicitly in his third *Antirrheticus*[36] that Constantine's soldiers dismissed by Irene in 786 had "wandered aimlessly as the planets" seeking an iconoclastic sect until they came to rest among the "Manichaeans", by which we must understand the Paulicians. Nearly a generation later, when some of the *tagmata*, recruited under the emperor Nikephoros I, broke into the Church of the Holy Apostles after the defeat of Michael I in 813 and spread the rumour that Constantine V had risen from the grave, Theophanes Confessor calls the instigators of the sedition Paulicians.[37]

The *tagmata* seem, therefore, to have contained a number of Paulicians in the late eighth and early ninth centuries. Theophanes relates that in the year 747 Constantine V moved Paulicians from Armenia to Thrace in order to strengthen the Bulgarian frontier with a reliable population[38] and according to Cedrenus some of the heretics even settled in the capital Constantinople. This transfer occurred after the capture of the cities of Melitene and Theodosiopolis (Erzerum) – Theophanes mentions in specific terms that – ....*ἐξ ὧν ἐπλατύνθη ἡ αἵρεσις τῶν Παυλικιανῶν.*[39] Constantine's favouring of the Paulicians is unmistakable. After the Iconoclastic council of 764, Theophanes wrote that the emperor Constantine was engaged in building cities (*πολίσματα*) in Thrace, to which he transferred Syrians and Armenians from the cities of Melitene and Theodosiopolis, giving them every assistance and rewarding them with gifts:

> *ταῦτα ἐπιτελῆ ποιήσας Κωνσταντῖνος ἦρξε δομεῖσθαι τὰ ἐπὶ Θράκης πολίσματα, ἐν οἷς οἰκίξει, Σύρους καὶ Ἀρμενίους, οὓς ἔκ τε Μελιτηναίων, πόλεως καὶ Θεοδοσιουπόλεως μεταναστὰς πεποίηκε, τὰ εἰς τὴν χρείαν αὐτοῖς ἀνήκοντα φιλοτίμως δωρησάμενος.*[40]

It was this favour shown to the Paulicians by Constantine that gave George, the monk, grounds for accusing the emperor of being a Paulician ...*οὐ γὰρ ἦν Χριστιανὸς ὃ μὴ γένοιτο ἀλλὰ Παυλικιανός.*[41]

Theophanes Confessor relates a curious legend about the emperor Constantine rising from his grave to give assistance to the beleaguered city. But he asserted that this legend was a fabrication of men who ...*σχήματι μόνον ἦσαν Χριστιανοὶ τῇ δὲ ἀληθείᾳ Παυλικιανοί*.[42] And the Bogomils who had been considerably influenced by the Paulicians regarded "Orthodox and right only the Iconoclasts, particularly Copronymus".[43] The favour shown to the Paulicians by the Isaurian emperors in this period would logically turn them towards Byzantium and against the Arabs. This change of attitude also had a more fundamental reason – a reason which demonstrates to a certain degree the national social and political aims of the Paulicians. Łewond, writing of a great revolt of the Armenian nobility under Grigor Mamikonean against the weakened Umayyad Caliphate in 784, says that certain rebels called "sons of sinfulness joined the rebel army".[44] Bart'ikyan[45] has convincingly identified these nameless "sons of sinfulness" with the Paulicians. As a result, the hostility of the Arabs against their former allies, the Paulicians, became even more acute.

In the second period of iconoclasm at Constantinople, the situation changed. Nikephoros I, considered by Theophanes as having shared the beliefs of the Paulicians, restored to the sectarians the full civil rights which they had lost during the iconodule reaction under the empress Irene. This period "allowed the Paulicians to live peacefully within the empire and to spread their doctrine".[46] This period of peace coincided with Sergius-Tychicus, the most able leader of the Paulicians from 801 to 835. During his 34 years of leadership of the movement Sergius gave a very distinct dimension to the sect, notably its martial character, because of which they suffered violent persecution from the Byzantine authorities, due not so much to the fact that from the standpoint of the Byzantine church they were heretics, as to the military and political menace which they represented to the empire.[47] Forming turbulent military colonies on the eastern borders of the Asiatic themes and frequently allied with the Arabs, the Paulicians were a serious threat. Under the leadership of Sergius, Karbeas and Chrysocheir, the sect staged open rebellions against Byzantium. The Paulician revolt coincided with the rebellion of the celebrated Thomas the Slav, and there is evidence that Paulician soldiers formed part of Thomas' army.

When empress Theodora initiated the reaction against the iconoclasts and finally triumphed over them, she issued a severe decree against the Paulicians as well. This is an indication of the fact that Paulicians co-operated with the enemies of Byzantium, both internal ones such as Thomas the Slav and external ones such as the Arabs. So, although it is true, as Lemerle[48] has shown, that Thomas' revolt was primarily motivated by personal and political hostility towards Michael II, and only to a lesser degree by any forms of general social and economic protest, this conclusion does not apply to the Paulicians. Their reason for supporting the rebellion would have been primarily political, a chance to achieve their social and political freedom.[49] For this reason, I do not think that Garsoian's objection to the thesis that the Paulician movement had political overtones could be proved wrong because Thomas' revolt was not political as such.

The Paulicians paid very heavily for their co-operation; about a hundred thousand Paulicians were executed in 844.[50] However exaggerated this estimate may be, it demonstrates clearly one point, namely that the Paulicians had become a serious vehicle of dissent. Karbeas, with five thousand of his coreligionists, settled in the lands of the emir of Melitene, who received him with honour and granted him sufficient lands on the upper Euphrates to build the cities of Argaous, Amara and subsequently Tephrike.[51] These cities became centres of Paulician military activities. The Paulicians once again allied with the Arabs and with their co-operation continued to organise raids on Byzantine territories, creating a state of constant war.

At the beginning of the reign of Basil I, the Paulician military power reached its apogee. Some thirty years after Sergius' death the Paulician armies, commanded by Chrysocheir, extended their domination to the Propontis and the Aegean Sea (869-870).[52] Basil I in 871 led the first campaign against them in person, which ended in disaster.[53] The heyday of the Paulician power was as short as it was spectacular. After the attempt to secure peace with them had failed, the Byzantine armies on their second attempt succeeded in 872 in finally crushing them. The Paulician military power was at an end. With the destruction of Tephrike the history of the Paulicians within the imperial provinces of the east comes to an end. Some of the sectarians acknowledged the imperial suzerainty while some left their fortresses and took refuge in the Balkans and in Armenia.

It seems strange that a single defeat in 872 destroyed the martial spirit of the sectarians, turning them into sectarians in the strictest sense of the term. But if we recall when and in what circumstances the T'ondrakec'i movement began, a number of unsolved issues become easier to understand. We showed at the beginning of this chapter, on the basis of the literary evidence, that the active persecution of the T'ondrakec'i sectarians began not later than the 70-80s of the ninth century. It only attracted the attention of the authorities when the movement absorbed more and more followers, becoming increasingly a serious threat both for the official church and the civil authorities. This sudden strengthening of the T'ondrakec'is gives us reason to suppose that some of the Byzantine Paulicians who had suffered defeat returned to their homeland and continued their campaign under the banner of the T'ondrakec'i movement. It seems very likely that this was so, because the regions in which the Paulicians spread most and were most effective were geographically very close to Armenia.[54]

This transfer of the Paulicians to Armenia was helped by another factor, namely that the majority of the adherents to the sects were Armenians. The sources show that the majority of the Paulician leaders were Armenians. Armenians always formed the majority in the provinces where the Paulicians were most influential and successful in spreading their doctrines. And most important of all, both the movements were very similar in character. In both, the lower classes formed its main strength. Under such circumstances it is obvious that the Paulicians would join the T'ondrakec'is and strengthen them. It is this union which gave Grigor Magistros the opportunity to identify the

T'ondrakec'is with the "Manichaeans" i.e. the Paulicians. This historical connection is also borne out by the title of the 67th letter in which it is stressed that the heretics who had approached the Syrian Patriarch were "Manichaeans" from T'ondrak and the "Land of the Greeks". The new inhabitants of *Šnavank'* referred to by Grigor Magistros in his letters were Paulicians who had fled from persecution and in co-operation with the T'ondrakec'is, were trying to achieve their common objectives.

There seems to be no ground for suggesting that the two movements were identical.[55] They were effective in different geographical settings, and originated from different historical factors. Paulicianism, particularly in the ninth century, was most effective and active in western Armenia which for centuries had been under Byzantine dominion, and as a result its social and economic life developed in a manner completely in line with Byzantine social and economic structure. The T'ondrakec'i movement, on the other hand, originated and spread in central Armenia, where there was a feudal system quite different from the social structure of Byzantium. In the ninth to eleventh centuries, as has been shown, Armenia had reached a peak of economic development.

Through the co-operation of the Paulicians with the T'ondrakec'is, the movement was revitalised and given a new social-political framework which had been a dominant feature of the Paulicians for two centuries. Clearly the T'ondrakec'is held views similar to the Paulicians but the fact that the former originated in Armenia proper independently of the Paulicians suggests that there were also differences between the two groups.

CHAPTER VI

SOURCES FOR THE STUDY OF THE ORIGIN AND THE DOCTRINE OF THE T'ONDRAKEC'I MOVEMENT

The Armenian sources relating to the T'ondrakec'i heresy consist of a sizeable body of documents covering the tenth to twelfth centuries, as follows:

(a) Treatises; (b) Chronicles; (c) Polemical letters.

Unfortunately, heretical literature has been badly handled by time and men. Its destruction by implacable and victorious opponents was a natural consequence of the spirit in which religious controversies were waged. So we learn most about them from the writings of those who sought to controvert heresy. The *Treatises* are composed of material useful for the defence of Orthodox doctrines and neglect the description of heresy or heretical arguments. The *Chronicles* are largely aristocratic, seeking to record the political and military fortunes of the noble families, and not the history of religious dissent. *Letters* are relatively abundant, especially for the eleventh and twelfth centuries. These heterogeneous data will be described in considerable detail, as the quality and the reliability of the sources vary.

From the ninth century, which is generally considered to be the period during which the sect of the T'ondrakec'is was developing in Armenia, we unfortunately possess no sources. By the end of the tenth century, however, the sect had become so powerful that many Armenian ecclesiastics were accused of the heresy. Among these may have been Grigor of Narek, and his uncle, the abbot Anania of Narek. Both men wrote doctrinal admonitions to known heretics. Anania's *Treatise against the T'ondrakec'is* (943-965), which contained the teachings and doctrines of the heresy and its refutation was the standard manual for all subsequent writers on the subject. Grigor Magistros, in his *Letter to the Syrian Kat'ołikos*, mentions "the writings of the holy and thrice-blessed *vardapet* Anania, which he wrote at the instance of the lord kat'ołikos of Armenia Anania (943-965), and also the writings of the lord Yovhannēs, the overseer of Armenia, whose names we have written in this letter; from these thou wilt see the truth about this evil beast . . . ".[1] Grigor in the same letter refers to the above work when he states: "so have our pontiff, the holy Yovhannēs and the *vardapet* Anania, branded these of today, and have described their wicked, horrible heresies".[2]

Similarly, Grigor of Narek in his letter to the heretical abbot of the monastery of Kčaw gives the summary of the above *Treatise* and concludes the section by confirming "These, then, are they whom my father's brother, a *vardapet* of great acumen, closely investigated, as being himself an apologist of God. And he, like a learned champion, and had he not done so we should hardly have known."[3] Grigor ends his letter with the recommendation "as to that well-informed book of the abbot Anania which with painstaking care he has written against these same sectarians, be sure to have it copied".[4] In the twelfth century Nersēs IV Šnorhali (1166/7-1172/3) refers explicitly to the above *Treatise* in his *Encyclical Letter.*[5]

In 1892 Galust Ter Mkrttschian published a document called *Gir Xostovanut'ean* or *Book of Confession* which he claimed was the presumed work of Anania of Narek[6], the famous *Treatise against the T'ondrakec'is* written by order of the kat'ołikos Anania Mokac'i and mentioned by Grigor Magistros, Grigor of Narek and Nersēs Šnorhali. However, from the very day of publication many scholars have objected to the claim. Karapet Ter Mkrttschian did not consider the document to be the *Treatise* of Anania of Narek for it does not have any specific information on the T'ondrakec'is nor does it have the features of a refutation.[7]

Those scholars[8] who agreed with G. Ter Mkrttschian have failed to consider the testimony of Grigor of Narek which clearly states the content of the *Treatise. The Book of Confession* published by G. Ter Mkrttschian does not in any way satisfy the description given by Grigor of Narek and Nersēs Šnorhali. The editor himself in his introduction confesses that the published document does not satisfy his expectations: "we knew that Anania of Narek had written a refutation against the T'ondrakec'is at the order of the kat'ołikos, and we expected a good deal of information, but we find nothing significant".[9]

Gir Xostovanut'ean is a doctrinal admonition, written by an Armenian priest accused of the heresy. In it he protests against the false accusation, anathematizes the T'ondrakec'is and all heresies, emphasising his orthodoxy by reciting the creed he believes in. Whether this work was written by Anania of Narek or not (or another priest of the same name), it demonstrates how dangerous the heresy had become, for even prominent clerics were thought to have been sympathetic towards the doctrines of the heresy.[10] The document published by G. Ter Mkrttschian is the treatise of an unknown Anania while the *Treatise against the T'ondrakec'is* "is probably no longer in existence".[11]

Fortunately Grigor of Narek in his *Letter to the abbot of Kčaw* "set down a few points out of many, little out of much" which his own uncle and teacher Anania of Narek "investigated" and like a "learned champion, radically demolished".[12] Thus

Grigor summarised the teachings and doctrines of the T'ondrakec'is in the following fourteen points. My notes are given in brackets.

Then among the observances which we know to have been repudiated by them as neither apostolic nor divine

(1) Ordination, which the Apostles received from Christ.

(2) The communion of His Body, of which the Apostle said by eating the bread thereof we receive and eat Himself in the flesh, and before which we tremble, Smbat calls a common meal.

(3) The birth through spiritual throes, of the water and spirit, which brings forth as had been preached children to God, concerning this, he had taught them to be nothing but mere bath water.

(4) And the blessed Lord's day, on which God the Word created the first light and perfected thereon the light of His rising (Resurrection) and on which finally He dispensed the light of His Life-giving Advent – this day, adorable for all it doth image, he hath taught them as being on a level with other days.

(5) Genuflexion in mysterious prayer, which Jesus Christ, Creator of all things, himself humbly observed.

(6) The fount is denied by them, in which Christ himself was baptized (Rejection of Baptism).

(7) The Communion of immortality, which the Lord of all things Himself tasted (The 6th and 7th points seem to repeat the 2nd and 3rd points in a slightly modified way).

They preach:

(8) The filthy habit of lecherous promiscuity, where the Lord forbade so much as a look.[13]

(9) They deny the venerated sign (i.e. the Cross), which God, made man, raised and carried on his shoulder as his own glory and authority.

(10) Their anthropolatrous apostasy, more abominable and cursed than idolatry (This may be a reference to their refusal to recognise divinity as part of Christ's nature).

(11) Their self-conferred contemptible priesthood, which is a likening of themselves to Satan (It appears that here, as in the first point, the reference is to the rejection of the Christian priesthood or hierarchy).

(12) Their deprecation of the sacrament of marriage, which, Our Lord in person, by a miracle, and in the company of his God-bearing Mother, prized and honoured. This sacrament they contemn, and reckon the mere fact of union in love with one another to be perfect love, and from God and pleasing to Christ; saying that God is love and desires the love union alone, and not the sacrament of marriage.

(13) Their railing and cavilling at the first-fruits, which Abel and Noah and Abraham and David and Solomon and Elias appointed to conciliate the Divine wrath.[14]

(14) We know how they dare to call the head of their abominable sect a Christ; of whom Christ testified beforehand, saying, "There shall arise false prophets" and this is the meaning of the prophet's saying: "The fool said in his heart, there is no God".[15] (Grigor of Narek makes the last point again in a different way in another context: "The foul Smbat, a second Simon, allowed himself to be worshipped by his disciples, men rooted in bitterness and sowers of tares; just like that wizard of Samaria".[16])

It is obvious that the fourteen points cited express the objections of the T'ondrakec'i heretics towards the authority of the Armenian Church's form of baptism, the eucharist[17] and marriage.[18] They did not admit such Orthodox practices as fasts[19], the offering of sacrifice[20], ordination of priests and celebration of holy days.

In addition to minor information in the same *Letter*, Grigor included in his book, of devotions a curious chapter describing the church, entitled *Discourse concerning the Church against the Manichaeans who are Paulicians.*[21] The chapter itself is purely descriptive and as such uninformative, but the identification of the Paulicians (T'ondrakec'is) with the Manichaeans, which we meet constantly in the Byzantine sources, such as Peter of Sicily, is repeated. In the *Letter* to the abbot of Kčaw this identification is not maintained except for a passing remark concerning the sectarians: "What gifts of election have they seen in the abominable Kumbrikios Mani".[22] Other heretics such as Simon Magus and Nestorius are also mentioned in the *Letter* as the forerunners of the T'ondrakec'is, so that no particular identification with Mani seems intended at this point. Furthermore, the doctrine described in the *Letter* has, as we have seen, very little which is consonant with any form of Manichaeanism.

Grigor of Narek's *Discourse concerning the Church against the Manichaeans who are Paulicians* is written in defence of the sacredness of the "visible church", which the T'ondrakec'is seemed to have objected to. In it Grigor gives a painstaking description of the various features of the church building, enumerates the function of each part of the church, in opposition to the T'ondrakec'i doctrine that the church was merely the gathering of the faithful. Grigor Magistros likewise asserts that the T'ondrakec'is "represent our Armenian worship of God as the worship of idols; as if we, who honour the sign of the Cross and the holy pictures, were still engaged in worshipping devils".[23] He quotes them as saying "We are no worshippers of matter, but of God; we reckon the cross and the church and the priestly robes and the sacrifices of the Mass all nothing".[24]

This belief is also noted by Nersēs Šnorhali, according to whom the heretics were accustomed to say: "The church is not the one which is built by man, but we ourselves".[25] The consequent rejection of church building is remarked by Paul of Tarōn, who writing in the early twelfth century states that the T'ondrakec'is "declared cross and church to be alien to the Godhead".[26] The evidence assembled indicates that the T'ondrakec'is, like their predecessors the Paulicians, were violently opposed to the cross and all form of reverence of images. "They destroyed it wherever they saw it, claiming that they were not worshippers of matter, but of God".[27]

In the eleventh century, the historian Aristakēs Lastiverc'i devoted two chapters of his *History* to the manifestations of the heresy of the T'ondrakec'is, thus providing us with what may be an eyewitness account.[28]

Chapter XXII *Concerning the evil heresy of the T'ondrakec'is which appeared in the province of Hark'*, contains a great deal of useful information mingled with the customary invectives and perorations. It tells us the story of a bishop named Yakopos who "had charge of the church of the family of Hark'",[29] i.e. was the bishop of the province of Hark'. This individual "at the beginning of his term of authority exemplified all the virtues. He dressed in sack-cloth, fasted, went barefoot; and he chose priests who always accompanied him, men coarsely clad and simple, who avoided a life of pleasure, and constantly occupied themselves in the singing of psalms". In short, a perfect representative of the Christian prelate.

And the fame of his exemplary life had spread far and wide and drawn the admiration of all near and far, so much so that "everyone was anxious to see him".[30] Even the haughty and overweening authorities of the province respected, honoured and obeyed him, so that "had he bid them draw their last breath, there was not one of them who would have opposed him, or have ventured to open his mouth and murmur".

After having been given such an excellent certificate of good conduct, bishop Yakopos' activities are without reason condemned as being "dangerous": "all this was hypocrisy and not sincere", they "disguise themselves under cover of our godly religion in order to deceive the simple minded, and by their soft words take captive the minds of the innocent". As a result of this invective which says nothing and, particularly, proves nothing, bishop Yakopos, contrary to all the previous recommendations, becomes: "the first-born satellite, then, father of all evils",[31] i.e. the first follower of Satan.

The accusations made against the bishop accomplished very little. On the contrary, what can be deduced from the accusations is that in order to eliminate the perversions and corruptions from within the church, the bishop had introduced certain reforms.

What were those reforms that are considered "incompatible" and "destructive poison" by the orthodox Aristakēs?[32] (1) "He began by establishing election among priests according to worth, and told the unworthy to keep silence". (2) "He ordered the worthy ones only to present Offering (or Masses) three times in the year". (3) And taught "that if a man has not in his own soul himself repented of his sins, then commemorations help him not, neither Offerings".

What is there in these three points that can be regarded as against and contrary to the prevailing standards of Christian practice? It must be presumed that the above reforms excluded the lucrative profits of the "unworthy", and more significant, since the church had become increasingly static and suspicious of new ideas as potential heresy, it could not help but disapprove of the reform measures which the bishop

Yakopos was trying to implement. For that reason there emerges a conflict, in which the church first condemned him, and then tried to convene a general council but failed, because as the historian reports, the authorities of the province were "all as it were spell-bound by his hypocritical demeanour, they declared that they would all die as it were by war, before they would give him into the hands of the council".[33]

Finding no other alternative, the church authorities turned to the common procedure in such situations – compelling their opponent to be more explicit. They sent to the bishop a priest by the name of Isaiah who, pretending to be his follower, established a very close relationship "but once he had studied and informed himself about the *Mcłnē*[34] cult of Yakopos . . . at once went and related the same to the holy patriarch Sargis". Which of Yakopos' teachings expressed his affiliation to the *Mcłnē* cult the historian does not record but that it was a mere slander, is evident since Yakopos, according to the same author, lived a very ascetic life.

The kat'ołikos of the day, Sargis I Sevanc'i "with gentle words" summoned Yakopos, "deprived him of holy orders, and branded his forehead with the image of a fox" proclaiming that "that will be the penalty and sentence for all those who join the fold of the T'ondrakec'is". Yakopos managed to escape and to take refuge in the province of T'ondrak. Aristakēs' account that he fled to Constantinople and sought "to be baptized according to their rites" (i.e. Greek) is altogether unfounded.

Nothing profoundly significant is communicated by Aristakēs in the subsequent chapter entitled *How in the borders of Mananaɫi there burst out a conflagration of folly.*[35]

In this chapter the author narrates the history of a certain monk Kuncik who had learned his T'ondrakec'i doctrines from a certain monk from Arrān. This Kuncik, "being a busy worker of Satan", captivated a certain woman, named Hranuš, and through her two sisters who were related to her family, and whose names were respectively Axni and Kamara, who "having caught the wild instinct of fornication, as is usual in their fold, proceeded with the cleverness of witches to make themselves Satan's teachers". These two made their two family estates the centre of their community, according to the historian, as "dens and lairs" for the sectarians, and in doing so became directly responsible for the further strengthening of the sect.

The historian then continues his history with the information concerning the brother of these "witches" a prince named Vrveř, who at the beginning, like the bishop Yakopos, was faithful to the creed and "foremost in all zeal for piety",[36] so much so that he had built a monastery on his own estate and gathered in it ascetic brethren. He supplied the brethren with all they needed, and their superior was known by the name of Andrew, who "was very famous for his zeal in all works of religion".[37] The historian testifies that the prince Vrveř every year during Lent visited the monastery and participated in their prayers till Easter, and also describes this prince as a person who "believes, listens, serves, hopes and loves".

But just as the bishop's conduct was defined as being "hypocrisy", prince Vrveř is defined as being: "the evil one inveigled these women, for they with the abandonment of passion fornicated promiscuously with him, without taking any account of their nearness of blood".[38]

Of course, the moral conduct of the T'ondrakec'i sectarians was very similar to that of the *Mcłnē*, in that they also rejected the orthodox form of marriage. The accusation of immorality on the part of the heretics is probably no more than the usual ecclesiastical propaganda that would result from the sectarian's refusal to recognise the authority of the Armenian orthodox clergy and recognise the sacramental value of a marriage performed by an orthodox priest.[39] This principle is at work in the shape of the twelfth accusation against the T'ondrakec'is referred to in the *Letter* of Grigor of Narek.

From these two chapters of Aristakēs Lastiverc'i just discussed, there is very little information regarding the doctrines of the sectarians. Only at the end of the chapter does Aristakēs Lastiverc'i, as a watchful prelate, announce:

> . . . But what is manifest about them and fit to be repeated is as follows: Church and church ordinances they utterly reject, its baptism, the great and awesome mystery of the Mass, the cross and the ordinance of fasts.[40]

In this period Mesopotamia included the southern Armenian districts of Vaspurakan and Tarōn, and Grigor Magistros carried on an active persecution of the T'ondrakec'is within his province.[41] His *Letters*, among them one to the heretics themselves and another to the kat'ołikos of Syria to whom they had appealed for help, have been preserved.[42] With Grigor Magistros we have again a first-hand informant who claims that his knowledge was derived from the confession of two recanting heretical priests who had acquainted him with the writings of one of their heresiarchs.

In the *Letters* he recites his exploits in bombastic manner. Like all apologists, Grigor also delights in defining his opposition in rude and inelegant language:

> This evil beast of prey, this bloodthirsty, sodomitic, whoring, lustful, frenzied, loathsome Smbat . . . Smbat the false-cleric, that has shaken the foundation of the apostles . . . that Smbat, who (just as dogs and wolves) began to teach all the sum of evil.[43]

In his *Letter to the T'ulaili*[44] mentioning the fact that the T'ondrakec'is have had the "impertinence" to appeal to the Armenian kat'ołikos, Grigor Magistros asks "Is it possible that you should think you can persuade him, who now occupies the patriarch's throne, to accept that for which more than fifteen pontiffs have anathematized you and your pack of dogs that have fallen victim to your beast of prey?" From here we know that the T'ondrakec'is as a movement were "anathematized" by fifteen Armenian pontiffs. In the same letter, however, we come across a passage which speaks of not fifteen but only thirteen pontiffs:

During 170 years have thirteen patriarchs of Great Armenia, as many of Albania, a myriad of bishops, and innumerable priests and deacons admonished you, spoke and confuted you, anathematized and proscribed you, and you have not repented.[45]

until at last the

Holy Ghost and the prayer of my ancestor and progenitor, St. Grigor, led me forth. And I came to Mesopotamia and encountered the deadly, stormy, muddy flood which, flowing forth from the cursed T'ondrakec'i Smbat, rolled death along in its waves.[46]

Grigor with great satisfaction records that after having wiped out the sectarians from Mesopotamia he set out for the place where the "viper and scorpion and dragon of wickedness had nestled", that is T'ondrak, which he devastated and left in ruins, as his ancestors had done to Aštišat (reference to Grigor I the Illuminator). After having recorded these historical facts, Grigor expresses the hope that as a result the sectarians would repent and recant their false teachings. This is followed by a threat that if they do not repent they should not attempt to "teach and confirm your evil heresy either by writing or by speech" otherwise "the might of God will find you out, and in his wrath and zeal He shall vex you".

First the author of the *Letter*[47] requests the Syrian kat'ołikos to find and read the writing of Anania of Narek, which he had written "at the instance of the kat'ołikos Anania (Mokac'i) and also the writing of the overseer of Armenia lord Yovhannēs (Yovhannēs Ōjnec'i) against the heresiarch Smbat of Zarehawan who has learned his evil erroneous teaching from a Persian physician and astrologer whom they called Mǰusik".

The first and most fundamental indictment brought against Smbat of Zarehawan is that he abandoned completely the apostolic tradition and rejected entirely the authority of the Armenian orthodox hierarchy. In the same letter the T'ondrakec'is were accused of being "idolators" and Grigor quotes them as saying: "We are not worshippers of matter but of God; we reckon the cross and the church and the priestly robes and the sacrifices of the Mass all for nothing".[48]

The second accusation is that having rejected the hierarchy of the church, Smbat himself "assumed the position of a high priest" and "in order to deceive and cajole the people they employ bishops secretly fallen away and excluded from the church to perform by night their worthless ordinations".

There is also the third accusation, which is stated in very general terms. They "hide their evil heresy" and never "reveal by any sign their nest of destruction, but to anyone who asks they point out another place and lead him astray".[49] According to Grigor Magistros, this was the reason why the Syrian pontiff was inadequately informed about the sectarians.

In addition to Smbat, Grigor Magistros lists as heresiarchs of the T'ondrakec'is: T'odoros, Ananes, Ark'ay, Sargis, Kiwreł (Cyril), Yesu and in his own time Łazar.[50]

For one hundred and seventy years these leaders remained loyal to their founder; in spite of having been anathematized by all patriarchs of Armenia and Albania. Concerning one of these leaders, Kiwreł, it is said that in order to discredit the church hierarchy and the eucharist he "took the paste, formed it in his hand, dipped it in the wine, and threw it away disrespectfully saying "This is the fraud of you Christians".[51]

The remaining section of the *Letter* is devoted to the activities of Grigor himself and his attempts to annihilate the movement. It presents the following picture. After having been appointed *dux* of Mesopotamia (1042-1055), he recognised the strength and power of the sect, accepted the confession of two recanting heretical priests and on the basis of their betrayal he organised an active and ruthless persecution of the T'ondrakec'is within his province; as he relates "I rooted out of the land the tares sown by them". Not satisfied with this, Grigor travelled to the village of T'ondrak where "the leaven of the Sadducees was buried, and the hidden embers of wickedness blazed", and acquiring special permission from the emperor, Constantine IX Monomachus, "I cleaned out the noxious growth of weeds".[52] As a direct result of these systematic persecutions many "confessed their guilt and errors", repudiated their leaders and were baptized in the church; "Those, however, who were baptized were over a thousand in number, nor did they cease to come to us for enlightenment" – relates Grigor with a great sense of achievement.

Grigor Magistros continues his account of the T'ondrakec'is and gives a great deal of useful information concerning the doctrines and practices of the sectarians:

> These are the crimes of these malefactors. No fasts are theirs, except out of fear; no differences do they observe between men and women, not even as regards the family, though they do not venture openly on this. They respect nothing, either of things divine or of things created; but laugh all to scorn, the old law as well as the new. When, however, you ask them openly, they anathematize and swear vehemently and deny.[53]

"Such was also the attitude of the Paulicians" writes Grigor, "who got their poison from Paul of Samosata. When we question them, they say: We are Christians; they are for ever chanting hymns and quoting the Gospels, and the Apostles, but when we ask: Why do you not allow yourselves to be baptized as Christ and the Apostles enjoined they answer: You do not know the mystery of baptism; we are in no hurry to be baptized, for baptism is death".[54]

"Similarly the sun-worshippers who are also known as *Arewordik'* (Sons of the Sun)[55] regard themselves as being orthodox, yet we know that you are aware what error and lewdness they practise. So are all those T'ondrakec'is who call themselves Kašec'i", and those T'ondrakec'is who are "in Xnus, who declared that Christ has been circumcised, and the T'ulaili who declared that he had not". There may have been many variations in their views but "I would have you know" concludes Grigor "that at heart they do not own him God, whether circumcised or not; but they only make of it a pretext for calumniating us".[56]

Then Grigor Magistros writes about the various T'ondrakec'i "Godless" leaders, namely Yesu, and the letters which he had collected from the various districts, which were full of "perversities of these devilishly minded men", but does not say concretely what these perversities were. Grigor makes a particularly interesting remark only when he names one of the heretical centres *Šnavank'* (Dog Monastery) in which "there lived men clad as monks and a multitude of whorish women. So we ordered their roof-trees to be thrown down and burned and their tenants to be hunted out of our marches".[57]

At the end of the letter Grigor Magistros warns the Syrian patriarch not to have any sort of relations with the sectarians; if any of them "confess to their evil deeds and wizardry" and condemn their "evil workers", such should be sent to him "so that they may come to us and receive baptism. In any other case thou shalt not have mercy upon them or have any communication with them or deign to look on them; but, like your fathers and brothers like-minded . . . curse them whenever they come into your mind".[58] Grigor Magistros on two other occasions refers to the T'ondrakec'is without specifically giving their name.[59]

In another of his letters[60] he writes that the T'ondrakec'is regarded the adoration of the cross and the holy pictures as being idolatry, "worshipping devils". The following passage from this letter is particularly interesting:

> And many of them spare not to lay hands on the church, on all priestly functions, on our awesome exalted sacrament of the divine body and blood. But all this derives from those scholars of the Manichaeans, who, having been utterly cut off from God, and having no hope of resurrection, are named T'ondrakec'is.

This particular passage stresses what we already know, namely that the T'ondrakec'is reject the church with its hierarchy and priestly functions and the sacrament of the Eucharist, understanding the bread and wine symbolically as the teaching of Christ in connection with the practice of "communal meals". But the particular combination of this passage is the insistence upon the Manichaean character of the heresy, associating the T'ondrakec'is with the Manichaeans.[61]

The violent persecutions instituted by Grigor Magistros do not seem to have had the successful results of which he boasted.[62] The T'ondrakec'is, far from being extirpated, fled in part to Syria, but were still flourishing sufficiently a century later to arouse the indignation of Paul of Tarōn[63] and the kat'ołikos Nersēs Šnorhali.

Paul of Tarōn (d.1123) in an epistle written against Theophistus, the Byzantine philosopher, refers to the T'ondrakec'is, although there is nothing in his testimony that adds to what we know about them from the previous sources. The passage relevant to our purposes reads:

> And it was not right for us to write at length, nor mention the T'ondrakec'is. Inasmuch as a kind which has not the witness to the faith, nor its foundations, nor God, had no need of the cross or of church.

> . . . the T'ondrakec'is then in their evil gainsaying declare that the sacrifice or *matał* is of no avail to the dead. And so we have found them to be on a level with these heretics, who oppose the sacrifice of Christ which is fulfilled because of sin. A certain Apellas[64], a filthy man and grown old in the flesh, soured by length of days and puffed up by devils . . .

Paul of Tarōn, in addition to associating the T'ondrakec'is with the Manichaeans, compares them to the Marcionites as well: "the Marcionites who do not admit the resurrection of the dead, and deny the holy sacrifice to be aught, and say that the God-receiving holy cross is mere wood, and have been blinded by the power hidden therein, just like these T'ondrakec'is".[65]

Among the Armenian sources Paul of Tarōn is the chronicler who specifically confirms that there was a link between the Paulicians and the T'ondrakec'is. He considers Smbat of Zarehawan to be a follower of Paulicianism when he states "thus behaved the *T'ondrakec'ik'* whom you call *Poplikianosk'* [sic]; they are disciples of the evil Smbat, he who got his poison from the sect of the Paulicians".[66] As Paul is addressing himself to a Byzantine it is safe to assume that by the twelfth century the Byzantines had identified the T'ondrakec'is with the Paulicians.[67] In connection with the Armenian sources concerned with the T'ondrakec'is it is interesting to note in the later period the appearance of the accusation of Manichaeanism also found in the Byzantine sources. Only late Armenian sources make this charge and even then not uniformly. No suggestion of Manichaean identification is found in the account of Aristakēs Lastiverc'i, but the accusation is made by Grigor of Narek, Grigor Magistros and Paul of Tarōn.[68]

Also from the twelfth century are the *Letters* of Nersēs IV (1166-1172).[69] Nersēs IV, although he no longer lived in Great Armenia but at Hṙomklay in Cilicia, where the seat of the Armenian kat'ołikosate had transferred after 1147, gives us a great deal of information about the T'ondrakec'is in his letters. His brother Grigor III Pahlavuni (1113-1166) imposed upon Nersēs the task of addressing a general letter to the Armenian inhabitants of Mesopotamia, describing the confession of the orthodox faith of the Armenian church, and contradicting the heterodox opinions of the T'ondrakec'is. Nersēs carried out his brother's command in such a successful manner as to silence those who were inimically disposed towards the church, and to restore peace and unanimity amongst the community there.

The priests of the province of T'lkuran were disputing among themselves on the question of Christ's divine and human nature. Some were inclined to emphasize that the divinity of Christ suffered humiliation and death with the human nature on the Cross, while others tended to preach that it was only the human nature that suffered persecution and death.

Again some admitted the offering of sacrifices for the dead, known as *matał* while others rejected it; some took the Christian teaching regarding paradise as being symbolic and not as literal truth. Nersēs observes that some accept the practice of honouring the cross, while others equated it to worshipping devils and idolatry.[70] We shall not here concern ourselves with the view of Nersēs Šnorhali brought in defence of the Armenian orthodox practices such as fasts, the offering of sacrifices, the sacraments – this would constitute a digression of limited relevance. But what cannot be overlooked is that Nersēs Šnorhali admonishes those who reject the orthodox sacraments and practices, the examples of Sabellius, Arius, Nestorius, Eutyches, Paul of Samosata, Apollinarius and others by saying the following: "You regard the suffering and the passion as being merely imaginary like the Manichaeans' [*Manikeac'woc'n*] profanity . . . neither the father took the form of a body nor the Holy Spirit, as Valentinus advocated impiously, but The Word became flesh". He refers to the Manichaeans once again when he writes: "therefore you think in the manner of the Manichaeans, for they first curse the food and then consume it", As regards the T'ondrakec'is Nersēs has this to say: "Henceforth we have heard, that some among the deceitful priests have begun to reiterate the filthy and impious teaching of the cursed Smbat T'ondrakec'i, causing ruin among the hearers".[71] Nersēs likewise says that the heretics were accustomed to say: "The church is not the one which is built by men, but we ourselves and the *Maštoc'*[72] and the practices it contains such as blessing the Cross and the church are not acceptable".[73] Nersēs Šnorhali himself does not make any attempt to refute the above accusations; he only affirms that several Armenian bishops have written and refuted them in the past, among them the famous treatise of Anania of Narek.

Also extremely interesting and worth mentioning is what Nersēs says about the sectarians. They are once again reiterating the teachings of Eutyches and the old heretics, when they state "the body of our Lord was not from the nature of man, but existed before the creation of man and before the ages in its divinity". In other words, Christ had brought his human body from heaven. The statement becomes even more significant when Nersēs refers to the analogy of the "water turned to ice" with which we are also familiar from Gnostic and heretical literature:

> Regarding those who say the existence of the word only was incarnated [coagulated] in the womb of the Virgin as water forming into ice, and not that it took its human nature and mixed it with his own, and this is the schism of Eutyches.[74]

Nersēs Šnorhali also wrote an epistle addressed to the Armenian clergy of the city of Samosata regarding the conversion of sectarians known under the appellation of *Arewordik'*.[75]

Before discussing the content of this letter it will not be out of place to mention the testimonies that exist in the sources regarding the Armenian sect, the *Arewordik'* or "Sons of the Sun", with whom the T'ondrakec'is were occasionally confused.[76] Grigor Magistros refers to the T'ondrakec'is as being the sun worshippers envenomed by these whom thev call the *Arewordik'*.[77] In his discourse *Sermon against the Paulicians* Yovhannēs Ōjnec'i mentions that the Paulicians of his time, in addition to associating with sun-worshippers and practising Persian sins, exposed the bodies of their dead.[78] In *The Book of Heresies*[79] it is reported that the Paulicians called the Sun the Christ. We find the same in the hymn of Armouris in the epic *Digenes Akrites*. This is regarded by several scholars as having been written in a Paulician environment. In the 200th line the following oath is found six times: "I swear by the sweet Lord Sun and his sweet mother".[80] It is interesting to note that the reflection of the above oath is found in the Armenian fable by Mxitar Goš (died 1214). It reads:

> La fleur du jonc et d'autres semblables furent accusées d'être des adoratrices du Soleil' Mais elle, élevant ses mains vers le Soleil, jura par le Soleil.[81]

In his letter to the clergy of Samosata Nersēs reports that the heretics who lived in the city and were called *Arewordik'* desired to be converted to the orthodox faith for "as by origin and language they are from the Armenian race, they aspire also to be one in faith and spirit". The representatives of the above sect had approached Nersēs and put their case before him. Nersēs states that he told them what he had read about their superstition and what he had heard about their evils committed by word and deed, from their own associates,[83] but does not specify what he had read. We know only that he compares them with the "Bogomils among the Romans (Byzantines) who like them have been deprived of the light of Christ's Gospel and remained in the darkness of paganism and ancestral superstitions. So also the Arewordik' part of our race have continued to remain in the darkness of Satan; they did not wish to be illuminated with the divine light through our Enlightener Saint Grigor, but instead preferred darkness to light until our time".[84]

Here, there is a question of old pagan beliefs which they wanted to reconcile with the Christian faith. The imposition of the Persian religion on Armenia during the latter part of the fifth century is known to all the chroniclers and provoked a major revolt of the Armenian nobility.[85] It may well have left in Armenia, particularly amongst the heterodox elements, some traces of sun-worship as well as other practices.

In *Dayl Ta'ril Dimasq* by Ibn al-Qalanisi[86] (555/1160) it is stated that the emir of Damascus Sihab ad-din Mahmud ibn Tugtekin (529-533/1135-1139) plotted against his commander-in-chief Bazwag.[87] He detailed a party of Armenian *Samsiyya*, who were members of his cortege to kill the commander in the citadel of Damascus. This adjective *Samsiyya* which means "of the Sun" is regarded as another name for the Arewordik'[88], the Armenian heretics related to the Paulicians and the T'ondrakec'is who were accused of worshipping the Sun and identifying Christ with the Sun.

A sectarian whose teachings bear a very close resemblance to those of the T'ondrakec'is appeared in the seventeenth century, around 1642. He was called T'omas J̌ułayec'i (of New Julfa). About him detailed information is preserved in Xač'atur J̌ułayec'i's *History of Persia*. Xač'atur, who lived a century and a half after the events he described,[89] records the following:[90]

> This occurred in 1091 of the Armenian era and in the year of Our Lord 1642, during the first reign of Shah-Sefi.

During this time there appeared a certain perverse and cruel (man) by the name of T'omas, who spoke profanity contrary to our orthodox belief in Christ, and who was more cruel and evil than Arius, Nestorius and the Sadducees.[91]

Xač'atur gives a summary of his teachings:

First, he did not accept the point that Christ is equal to God the Father, but taught that Christ was a mere man and that the Holy Virgin Mary was the bearer of a man.

Second, like the Sadducees he did not recognise resurrection and judgment.

Third, the Cross of Christ, the Mass and the Holy communion he rejected like the Mohammedans.

Fourth, the established Apostolic canons, the divine ordinances and the seven sacraments of the Holy Church he dishonoured.

Fifth, the prelates, vardapets, priests and the ministers of the holy church he ignored and called them deceivers.

And in this manner this cruel and evil man desired to introduce a new and most evil heresy into the Church of Christ.[92]

There is no doubt that the tenets of this movement appearing in the seventeenth century resemble those of the T'ondrakec'is. But Avdalbēkyan's opinion that the ideas of T'omas are more "radical since he rejects all the sacraments and the old canons of the of the church", goes too far. As the sources testify, the T'ondrakec'is also held similar views on the sacraments. Avdalbēkyan's suggestion that the T'ondrakec'is did not object to the idea of the resurrection of the body and the last judgment ignores the sources. He bases his view on the fact that Lastiverc'i and Grigor of Narek in their accusations do not say that the T'ondrakec'is rejected the resurrection of the body and the last judgment, so when T'omas openly states his objection to the above doctrines, Avdalbēkyan concludes that "the heretic of New-Julfa stands out as the only preacher of a movement which is most radical in the history of the Armenian heretical movements". Avdalbēkyan has failed to take into consideration the remark of Grigor Magistros regarding the T'ondrakec'is, namely that they "had no hope of resurrection".[93] Paul of Tarōn also talks of "the Marcionites who do not admit the resurrection of the dead . . . just like these T'ondrakec'is".[94] The T'ondrakec'is also rejected the doctrine of the belief in the resurrection. It is not clear how these T'ondrakec'i views and doctrines survived through the centuries and reached T'omas J̌ułayec'i.

The history of the Paulicians is clearer than their doctrines, which "must remain largely a matter of conjecture".[95] Among various, sometimes conflicting, reports are these: that they believed in two independent principles or deities; that they considered Christ to be a man adopted by God and filled with the Holy Spirit; and that they rejected the Old and some of the New Testament, repudiated Christian sacraments, and practised a vigorous iconoclasm. The Greek sources present them as dualists, teaching a Docetic doctrine of Christ (that his body was of a celestial substance). From time to time scholars like Conybeare have questioned this view on the basis of the Armenian sources. The Armenian sources depict them as Adoptionists, who accepted the unity of God, attributed all creation to Him, and denied the divinity of Christ. Both groups of sources emphasize the iconoclasm of the sect.

Garsoian, in presenting the history of Paulicianism, confirms some of Conybeare's conjectures. She does this on the basis of her analysis of the Greek and Armenian sources. Since the Armenian sources, most of whose authenticity is beyond doubt, almost without exception do not mention dualism in connection with the Paulicians, she concludes that the testimony of the Armenian sources should not be rejected but must be reconciled with the Greek evidence. Despite the statement in the text that it was written by a man who had served as an imperial legate in 869 to the Paulician capital, Garsoian is convinced that the history by Peter of Sicily is a mid-tenth century compilation which drew upon a variety of sources from diverse periods. Thus, the Byzantine cornerstone for the theory of Paulician dualism was compiled nearly a century after the heresy had ceased to be a major threat to the empire. And since the history was dedicated to a Bulgarian bishop, the work's concern with dualism could easily be attributed to the appearance in the tenth century of the Bogomil dualist heresy in Bulgaria — a powerful movement of dissent in the medieval history of Eastern Christendom.

Then she considers the testimony of the Armenian sources, the most important of these being *The Key of Truth*. Since the doctrine described in *The Key of Truth* is similar to that attributed to the Paulicians in medieval Armenian sources, Garsoian, like Conybeare, believes this to be an authentic text. The movement, a survival of an early Adoptionist trend, originated in Armenia, and its name may well be derived from Paul of Samosata. On the basis of this document she concludes that there were two groupings of Paulicians – in Armenia and in the Byzantine empire – representing the two doctrinal traditions. Ancient tradition was "characterized by the belief in the humanity of Jesus and his eventual adoption as Son of God upon baptism. This fundamental dogma was attended by the belief that ordinary men could also become the equals of Christ and worthy of adoration. This Armenian Paulicianism was characterized by violent iconoclasm and showed no apparent modification throughout the Middle Ages".[96] The main thesis is that Armenian Paulicianism remained static. In Byzantium, on the other hand, a change in dogma took place in the mid-ninth century, possibly under the influence of the great heresiarch Sergius and his successors. The original doctrine of the sect which had been similar to the one existing in Armenia, was gradually transformed into a docetic and dualist one. The traces of dualism among the Paulicians are interpreted either as a product of internal development or as a relatively late influence from extremists among the Byzantine iconoclasts.

Lemerle, in his review of Garsoian's study, considers her theory of the Greek sources to be far from his own and remains unconvinced.[97] The same could be said of her analysis of the Armenian *The Key of Truth*. The main thesis of Garsoian, which postulates "two traditions" for the history of the doctrine of the Paulicians, depends entirely on her acceptance of *The Key of Truth*, the content of which she brings into "essential agreement with the polemical sources". She underlines the fact that the doctrinal divergencies from Paulicianism that *The Key of Truth* presents must not prevent us from seeing this resemblance.

It is true that there is theological similarity between the doctrine of *The Key of Truth* and of the T'ondrakec'is. For example, the passage on (p.19) "You [the unbelievers] . . . are followers of your father, the evil one, who gave you his law, namely to baptize unbelievers, to worship images, to make silver and gold in the form of an image . . . and to adore the same"[98] is specific rejection of images and of the reverence of them as idolatry. Instead only "the mediation of our Lord Jesus Christ" is acknowledged and "not any other holy ones, either of the dead, or of stones, or of crosses and images" (pp. 53, 59-60) "for they need the intercession of the living and not the living theirs". "While the heretics and the schismatics [the Christians] during their liturgy for all whether priests, or deacons, or scribes, that is, apostles, saints, prophets, doctors, martyrs, patriarchs, monks, virgins, recluses, and of all saints, let there be, we pray, commemoration in the holy oblations" (p. 59). On page 53 it is maintained that true religion or piety is against the worship and veneration of "images, stones, crosses, waters, trees, fountains, and all other vain things; as they [the Christians] admit, and worship them, so they offer incense and candles". Likewise they did not admit such orthodox sacraments as "confirmation, the order of the priesthood, the last unction, and marriage, are not salvation of our souls. They are unnecessary and not obligatory".[99]

On the other hand, in the same *The Key of Truth* there are theological and liturgical statements, which are diametrically opposed to the T'ondrakec'i tenets.[100] We stressed earlier in relation to T'ondrakec'i doctrine that the heretics completely and categorically rejected all sacraments of the church, penance, baptism, communion, marriage and all the orders of the church.[101] But in this manual on pages 117-119 these very same sacraments are considered as being among the commandments of Our Lord Jesus Christ: "repentance, baptism (which is not for infants) and communion"; and on page 119 we read: "Four are they which save Man. First repentance; second right faith, third holy baptism, and fourth the holy precious body and blood of our Lord Jesus Christ". Having rejected the baptism of catechumens, to the question: "Then whose baptism and communion is valid?" the reply was: "Their holy baptism and communion only is valid who have original and operative sin" (p.118). Far more significant and remarkable is the interpretation of the sacrament of the Eucharist. The sacrament receives such a mystical and spiritual exposition that under no circumstances can it be reconciled with the T'ondrakec'i teaching. The T'ondrakec'is regarded the sacrament of the communion as being a "communal meal"; yet in *The Key of Truth* the concept of transubstantiation is discussed and developed in its most classic form. This is how the document has it:

> That our mediator and intercessor Jesus Christ, the lamb of God, took the bread in his hands, and blessed it, this the holy evangelists declare. That is to say he earnestly besought the almighty Father that He would change bread into his true precious body. This is why it says: "He blessed", that is, he prayed the Lord that

he would change the bread truly into his body. And so it was assuredly changed by the spirit of the heavenly Father. And when he saw that the bread was changed into His body, then He thanked the almighty Father for having changed it into his body and blood.[102]

The Key of Truth teaches the conversion of the whole substance of the bread and wine into the whole substance of the Body and Blood of Christ, effected by the elect one. No T'ondrakec'i would have given the sacrament such a mystical exposition.

Similarly our survey of the sources showed that the T'ondrakec'is entirely rejected the practice of ordination (laying on of hands) and election of clergy; but in *The Key of Truth*, chapter XXII is entitled "And concerning the order of laying on of hands".[103] At the ceremony of ordination the elect one presides, but the bishop is the one who lays hands on the candidate (p.10). At the beginning of the ceremony the candidate whom *The Key of Truth* designates as "Reader" and "Seeker", receives an ordination name "in accordance with the gospel" (p.107) after which "authority" is conferred upon him in these terms: "Take to thyself authority of binding and loosing the sons of men in heaven and earth" (pp.107-8).[104] This confirms that *The Key of Truth* emphasized both the importance of election and the sacraments of ordination, and that contrary to what is suggested[105] *The Key of Truth* does accept the existence of a recognizable heirarchy, though very different from that of the official church.[106]

On both internal and external evidence *The Key of Truth* is a document highly interpolated, subjected to revisions and alterations, on the basis of which we cannot form a true picture of the T'ondrakec'is.

Caution should therefore be exercised in using this text to reconstruct the ancient form either of Paulicianism or T'ondrakianism. To assert on the basis of *The Key of Truth* that Armenian Paulicianism underwent no changes is to beg the question. To say, in order to explain the differences, which amount to contradictions, between this Armenian Paulicianism (presented by *The Key*) and Greek Paulicianism, that the latter changed and developed during the eighth and ninth centuries, while the former remained static, is questionable. We cannot be sure that the beliefs of the Armenian Paulicians had not evolved considerably since the Middle Ages and that *The Key of Truth* was not a presentation of those evolving views. Garsoian, who persuasively argues that Paulician views and beliefs underwent a variety of changes in Byzantium, should be equally willing to consider that Armenian doctrine also was not static. Garsoïan's affirmation (also arising from her analysis of *The Key*) that one could present a coherent picture of the sect by seeing a certain continuity between the Paulician and T'ondrakec'i movements is not plausible. The fact that the T'ondrakec'i movement originated in Armenia independently of the Paulicians and in different circumstances suggests that there were also two distinct sects. These people clearly had views similar to the Paulicians but the fact that they split and presented themselves under two different names implies that there were two different sects, whose connections must be proved rather than assumed.

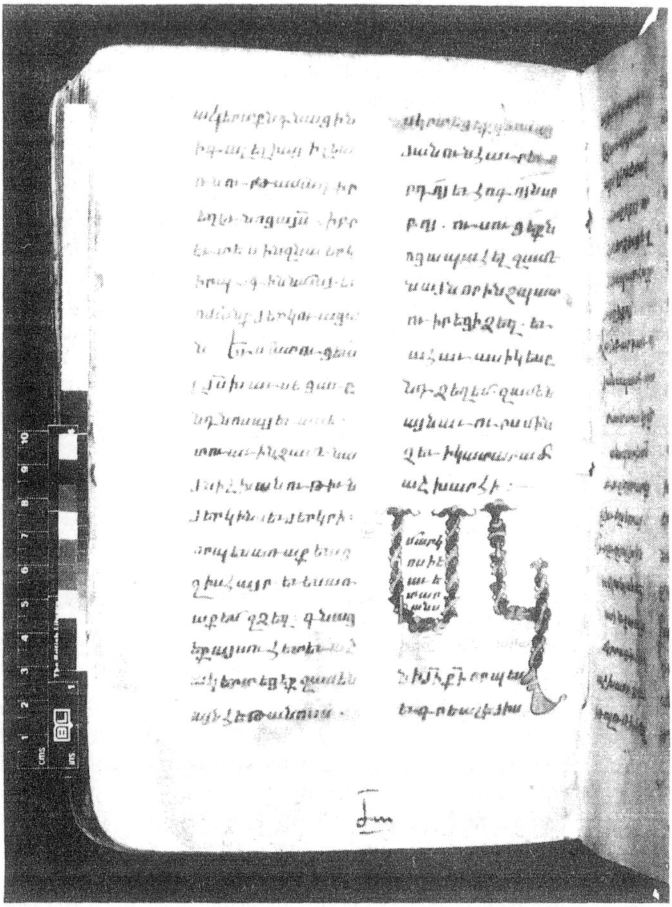

Armenian Manuscript THE FOUR GOSPELS. The Gospel of St. Mark. The British Library MS Or. 2678.

CHAPTER VII

THE T'ONDRAKEC'I MOVEMENT: SOCIAL, POLITICAL, OR RELIGIOUS?

The most stubborn problem in any discussion of heresy has been to trace and to discover the original root and inspiration. Among the numerous explanations advanced for the rise and spread of the medieval heresies the one most frequently encountered is that they were a product of resentment against a "corrupt" clergy in a church that had become wealthy, worldly, and forgetful of its mission. The church, relying on the approach taken by the Christian fathers from the second to the fifth centuries, covered all heresies under a blanket of moral condemnation, as a species of disobedience. Such a moralising view, unqualified by considerations of circumstances or historical development and applied equally to early as well as medieval heresies, is a serious distortion. The heresies of the Middle Ages went through mutations that are incomprehensible without reference to the changing circumstantial background.

Another theory is that heresies are essentially religious phenomena. The various heretical movements and groups that swept through Byzantium and Europe in the second half of the Middle Ages must be considered as individual manifestations of the religious fervour of those centuries. They may be called popular or pragmatic heresies because they took the forms of movements, putting into practice a collective variety of spiritual and ascetic activity, although they expressed religious experience in ways beyond the limits of what was then permitted in the catholic church and in opposition to its authority and to its dogmatic and moral teachings. Thus they are treated as independent deviations from the doctrinal norms of the church. According to this interpretation the heresy originates in the mind which, confronted with unfamiliar data to be absorbed rebels when it sees that those data do not conform with the ideals it already holds as the products of experience or education. The dissent of heresy in the Middle Ages therefore arose from the confrontation of men with dogma in the Christian faith which some felt they could not accommodate without self-betrayal. They passed this discontent to others pointing out the ideal standard of conduct or belief which the Christian society or its authorities were ignoring. In other words, heresy of the period in question is viewed as being a consistent striving after the ideal, after a religious and social pattern which the church and the state had failed to recognise.

The last interpretation of heresies arises from the question: were religious movements only convictions of mind, without reference to environment and material conditions? This theory presents heresies as being protests, expressed in religious terms, against socio-economic disruptions and inequalities. The ideologies of religious movements are forms of consciousness with which certain groups react to social or economic changes, or in which they express, in ideological terms, the class conflicts and struggles that arise from these changes. During the Middle Ages, ideological expressions of class struggles took predominantly religious forms, for the church dominated the whole superstructure of society with its dogmas and institutional organisations. So alienation from the church for these reasons is presumed to have opened the way for such doctrines as religious dualism, which explained good and evil by dividing creation between principals or gods of spiritual and material realms.

In specific instances of radical dissent one or other of these causes may be found to be dominant, but none of them alone is sufficient to explain the whole range of heretical movements in the Middle Ages. This is particularly true with regard to heresy in the Armenian church, given the church-centred character of Armenian life. Since the Armenian church was and is the only single major institution which guided and influenced practically every aspect of Armenian life, the distinction of the religious from the secular is very hard to discern. Religion was so vital an element of life that sectarian movements could not have been treated as casual or gratuitous matters. However it is also very difficult to say categorically that the Paulician or the T'ondrakec'i movement was either socio-economical or political as there is no adequate evidence to support such an interpretation. But one can trace how this particular movement was related to the history of Armenia in the ninth to eleventh centuries.

The period in question, starting with the development of an independent Bagratid kingdom until its conquest by the Seljuqs, coincided with a remarkably rapid cultural and economic expansion of the country and a great flourishing of its urban centres. The accounts of contemporary historians, the large number of extant monuments, information furnished by inscriptions, all bear witness to this period. In the second chapter I have tried to explain the basis for this cultural and economic progress. It is generally accepted that Armenia's economy and culture attained an exceptionally advanced level of development.

It is in this context that many modern Armenian historians have studied and evaluated the T'ondrakec'i movement, in terms of its being a proletarian movement in revolt against the intolerable oppression of a feudal society. It formed the ideological basis of the "Armenian Renaissance". In the rest of this chapter we shall try to state the evidence for such a conclusion. That such oppression did exist is beyond doubt. From the accounts of contemporary writers it is not difficult to see that the process of economic development, extension of monetary economy, accumulation of wealth in the cities brought with it brutal exploitation of the lower classes of the population. Aristakēs Lastiverc'i and Grigor Magistros give us definite information concerning the events which took place during the reign of Gagik I (990-1020). In his description of the pillage of the city of Arcn by the Seljuqs in 1049, Aristakēs Lastiverc'i relates that:

> Here was set up a law on growth and tithes and surtax on grain; the land is polluted by this and at the present time impediments are set in the way of those bringing the fruits of the earth to feed the people. He who deceives his friend boasts that he is wise and he who robs says that he is mighty. The wealthy have seized the houses of their unprovided relatives and the boundaries of their fields.

The same author, speaking of the capture and destruction of the city of Ani in 1064, notes particularly in it the presence of usury and social unrest:

> Because of the excess of injustice which took place in it, a mighty and beautiful palace was burned down and all of its buildings were reduced to a heap of earth, and the licentiousness and evil which had occurred in it came to an end. This is the lot of unjust cities which are built on the blood of others and which grow rich at the expense of the homeless, of those who toil in the sweat of their brow; they build their houses on luxury and the infringement of rights, they seek for themselves pleasure and profit having no pity in their souls for the poor and the homeless, withdrawing not from evil deeds, because they are possessed by their passions.[1]

In the last days of the Armenian kingdom in Ani before the invasion of the Turkish tribes, as has justly been shown by N. Marr, the life of feudal Armenia presented the antithesis of the economic oppression of the Armenian working population with the accumulation of wealth in the hands of a few members of the ruling classes. The Armenian historian, Matthew of Edessa, gives us interesting information concerning enormous wealth in the hands of the clergy at least. At the time of the taking of the city of Arcn by the Selǰuq general Ibrahim he writes that:

> . . . the treasures of the chorepiscopus Dawt'uk were seized by Ibrahim. His treasures were loaded on forty camels. From his house eight hundred ploughs with six pairs of oxen apiece went forth for the ploughing.[2]

During this period the wealth and number of churches and monastic establishments doubled.[3] During the reign of Abas I (928-953) the churches of Kamrǰajor, Hoṙomoc', Glajor, Tat'ev, Narek and several others were completed. During the reign of Ašot III (953-977) the monastic complexes of Sanahin and Haɫpat were completed. Asoɫik testifies: "The monastic establishments prospered and flourished. And in many places new monasteries were being constructed".[4] From the fourth century the newly established monastic and religious institutions were supported financially by the state which ceded to the church extensive lands. Through the centuries the acquisition of landed property constantly increased and formed the most profitable economic source and power of the church. During the period under discussion, and with the rise of feudalism, another source of income was the donations made by the rich to the church. These donations consisted of both movable and immovable property, to which the architectural monuments of the epoch bear eloquent witness.

In the canons of St. Sahak the kind of donations and the reason for them is clearly stated. Canon 51 states: "princes [give] their villages, estates, and treasures of gold and silver . . . some for their own salvation, some for their beloved and parents for the salvation of their soul . . . ".[5] However the donations made with these specific intentions are confined to the fourth and fifth centuries. In the ninth and tenth centuries the picture was completely different. In 901 a certain prince of Siwnik', Grigor Suban, reconstructed the famous Makenoc' monastery destroyed by Babāk and built two additional churches. The inscription stone states: "I, Suban, a prince of Siwnik', built the Makenoc' monastery and unsparingly decorated it with expensive vessels and Holy Testaments, and ceded our own property to it . . . ".[6] In 979 Smbat Bagratuni presented to the monastery of Sanahin "landed property consisting of several villages, farms . . . ".[7] In 1183 the prince Ivanē Ōrbelean gave to the monastery of Sanahin all his family estates.[8] The most outstanding was the accumulated wealth of the monastery of Tat'ev.

So in the first half of the eleventh century there was in Armenia a sharp contrast between the economic depression of the working population and the accumulation of wealth in the hands of a few members of the ruling class, the church and the clergy. How did the lower classes react? In the chronicles of this period we find several references to peasant uprisings. According to the testimony of Yovhannēs Drasxanakertc'i. ". . . the lower classes wished to be more competent than the upper class, and the servants planned, Solomon-like, how their masters should wear sandals and go on foot and how they themselves should sit on magnificent and prancing horses. They became proud, insolent and raised a great rebellion". The same author describing a rebellion on the borders of Armenia involving the neighbouring Greeks and the Armenians, adds that: "[To this revolt] also joined mischievous thieves and evil-doers and waged war on our land; but what was most disturbing was that on their path they came across churches which they defiled and left in ruins". This seems to be an oblique reference to popular dissent directed against the church which at this period was picking up momentum. "Brother against brother", says the historian, "fought each other destroying the country, cities and villages".[9] This destruction lasted for seven years (910-917). The kat'ołikos Anania Mokac'i when praising the achievement of king Abas simultaneously notes that he "executed the mischievous thieves and evil-doers".[10]

There is evidence that similar revolts were staged in the province of Siwnik', where the villagers refused to cede their lands and attacked the monastery. The historian Ōrbelean recounts the events of this period and stresses that the mob did not even refrain from destroying the containers in which the holy chrism was stored. This act was to the official church a sign of heresy, and the author who had previously called the attackers *mischievous thieves, bandits, evil doers,* now calls them *ungodly*. This rejection of the holy chrism betrays the link that existed between the dissidents and the sect of the T'ondrakec'is, for Grigor Magistros also comments that the T'ondrakec'is "disdain and mock the holy oil which is distributed by their leader".[11]

Ōrbelean confirms that in the eleventh century the peasants of several villages, which had been bought by the monastery of Tat'ev, revolted more than once, refused to cede their lands, and attacked the monastery. St. Ōrbelean's account is very interesting: "The peasants of the Makenoc' villages seized Gełark'uni and Vayoc'-jor where they appointed a bishop . . . but the lord Yovhannēs returned and suppressed those who had revolted and condemned those who had indulged in the preaching of false doctrines. With the co-operation of the pious king Vasak the villages were returned to the monastery".[12] This is also a reference to the T'ondrakec'i movement, particularly to those high-ranking clergy who had supported the sect and fought the owners of the monastery of Tat'ev by setting up their own centres and spreading T'ondrakec'i ideology, for which the kat'ołikos Yovhannēs V condemned them for being *evil-doers, foreign, wolflike prelates*. The fables of Vardan Aygekc'i contain information to the effect that "the love of God had diminished in our hearths"; that men "dislike praying" and the believers "refrain from the church, the cross, the gospels, the priests, the prayers and the fasts" and instead "spit on the cross and the church" claiming "there is no God". This is the attitude of not only the "lower" [i.e. peasants] but also of the "higher" [i.e. the nobles].[13]

Without directly mentioning the T'ondrakec'is, Xosrov Anjevac'i, father of Grigor of Narek, has the sectarians in mind when he writes: "Where they are influential they give respect to the church but where they are harsh and ungodly they also behave in the same manner. For from among the villagers they elect their ministers and not from God [i.e. the church] . . . ".[14] This particular testimony of Xosrov Anjevac'i is very interesting as regards the nature and character of the movement. It provides direct evidence of the peasant background of the sect. Aristakēs Lastiverc'i has also a valid point to make regarding the wide popularity of the T'ondrakec'i movement: "For their words eat into such (referring to the simple-minded) like a cancerous growth, and just as this is difficult to heal, so those who are taken by them can with difficulty keep themselves safe".[15]

These testimonies clearly indicate that in the tenth to twelfth centuries there was growing discontent among the people. The originator of the theory of an Armenian renaissance, Č'aloyan concluded that: "the renaissance is the result of the primary accumulation of capital; it comes to maturity during the last stages of capitalist production. It is quite understandable that the renaissance reflects the social and class struggle of the masses in the first period of the accumulation of capital, an altogether original struggle both in form and content. The highest stage of the culture of that society, that is, the renaissance, though secular in form, appears to be, in its content, a revolutionary movement opposed to ruling feudal ideals".[16] In order to defend his thesis, Č'aloyan cites the dissent of the T'ondrakec'i movement which supported the masses who were eager to throw off the church's yoke. Połosyan, who describes the object of his study as being "to analyse, on the basis of the available evidence, the social and economic state of the Armenian peasant and his struggle against his exploiters during the period from 850-1230"[17] declares that "one of the main characteristics of the history of the Armenian people during this period extending from the ninth to the thirteenth century is the acute and active form taken by the class struggle".[18] As a proof of the existence of the class struggle, frequent mention is made of the T'ondrakec'i movement. Soviet Armenian scholars fit into the pattern of the class struggle all previous sectarian movements such as the Borborites, Messalians and Paulicians.

As far as the actual outbursts and peasant rebellions which can be said to have resulted from the class struggle are concerned, they are limited to the few incidents mentioned in the works of contemporary Armenian history, such as the peasant uprisings in the villages of Tamalek, Berd or at the neighbouring villages of Tat'ev in Siwnik' at the beginning of the tenth century. But to present such incidental events as an "acute form of class struggle" and "as a general rebellion of peasantry" in a country with a peasant population of over four million souls – as Połosyan himself states – is a gross exaggeration.

The question is whether it is admissible to identify religious sects with social movements? Garsoian considered the validity of the above assumptions in the formulation of the social thesis on the Paulician - T'ondrakec'i movements.[19] "In a sense . . . the proletarian thesis is the least substantial" and cannot be sustained in the sources. Much of the thesis derives from the "principle of guilt by association". The Paulician–T'ondrakec'is were said to be dualists and their rejection of matter as evil was but an expression of the heretics' hatred of worldly goods and of the power of those who possessed them. Such an argument leads necessarily to the conclusion that religious sectarians are recruited exclusively from the lower classes. Garsoian shows that Paulicianism-T'ondrakianism was present in all classes of society.[20] The Armenian sources speak of prominent T'ondrakec'is: ladies of leading families and mistresses of villages, bishop Yakopos of Hark', and prince Vrveṙ of Širi.[21] The rural setting of the sects need consequently not derive exclusively from a peasant background or a love of the simple life, but from considerations of safety and necessity.

These two arguments of Garsoian are valid but at the same time one cannot, as the author does, ignore the social and political factors that won adherents for the movement. The presence of converts to the sect from the upper ranks of society is not an argument against the social thesis. The Paulicians, the T'ondrakec'is and other heresies like the Bogomils in Bulgaria caused the greatest stir because they had deeply held convictions which won adherents among the laity as well as the clergy. In Armenia the

Christian church had been from the beginning a part of the aristocratic establishment.[22] After the official conversion of Bulgaria to Christianity, an Eastern Orthodox Christian establishment was added to the existing secular establishment, and the burden imposed on the peasantry was increased proportionately. In twelfth century Languedoc, the masses were eager to throw off the church's yoke, while the nobles were eager to seize the church's property. This alliance of the nobles with the masses made Catharism in Languedoc potent.[23] The dissenting religious communities were bound to assert themselves in the most vigorous way in cases in which they won the support not only of a suppressed peasantry, but also of some of the members of the establishment.

The second of the Paulician heresiarchs on east Roman ground, Symeon, was an imperial official, and in the mid-ninth century their adherent Ližix was a member of the central bureaucracy with the probable rank of *proto – secretis*.[24] When in the ninth century the Byzantine state resumed its persecution of its Asiatic Paulicians, the Paulicians' two most famous and successful military leaders in their counter offensive were both of them former Byzantine officials. Karbeas was a staff officer of the commander-in-chief of the army, while his successor John Chrysocheir was a *spatharios*.[25] The Bogomils, whose original adherents had been recruited among the oppressed and unsophisticated peasantry in Bulgaria, won signal success on two occasions on which the sect gained converts in the upper ranks of society.[26]

These facts show that it would be unrealistic to ignore the secular motives for adhesion to T'ondrakianism, Bogomilism, and Catharism. The sects would never have come to anything, and therefore would never have alarmed the establishment if their adherents had not been inspired by convictions and enthusiasm strong enough to move them to risk punishment and, in the last resort, the death penalty, rather than recant. The link between the social and the religious sides of the dissenters was their deep concern with the problem of evil and social injustice. The grinding pressure of taxation, the social injustices of the widening gulf between the rich and the poor, and the devastation caused by the Arab raids, would be enough in combination to convince the victims of these tribulations that the world was evil and that it must be the handiwork of evil creator.

The appearance and development of the T'ondrakec'i movement within the framework of medieval Armenian religious and secular history should be seen as part of the general revival, economic and cultural, whose origins can be discerned as early as the eighth century. Its emergence coincided with the defeat of the Paulicians on the one hand, and the expressions of vitality in such diverse forms as expanding commerce, new social forms, and rise of cities on the other. Investigation of the social and economic setting in which the sect appeared has not produced satisfactory explanations of their origin in material terms. Yet religion had everywhere, particularly in the Armenian context, a great impact on daily life, and at the same time the expression of religious aspirations was strongly influenced by social origins. The advocating of a return to apostolic times, the preaching of poverty, the intention to free the church from its enslavement to worldly ambition and wealth, protest against the authority of the hierarchy, against the abuse of sacraments, corruption among the clergy, are all factors which could arouse the emotions and fervour of the laity, who became active participants.

The reception of the sect may partly be explained by the extent to which its teaching encouraged the expression of religious ideals. The non-theological aims of the T'ondrakec'is inspired panic in the hierarchy of the church and the secular rulers. This was mainly because the convictions of the movement coincided with those of the masses and were in some measure connected with popular upheaval. The T'ondrakec'i movement was successful because it involved a cross-section of society, including noblemen, leading citizens, even the upper privileged clergy. Grigor Magistros stresses the link between the T'ondrakec'is and the masses when he considers the sectarians as being an "obscure race, multitude", etc. Answering the question of the heretics that "they are being persecuted for a grudge", Grigor Magistros asks: "If they be of us and of our creed, what is there to grudge them? What academy or doctrine? What famous men, bishops and fathers, what great cross-bearing brotherhood? What monks withdrawn together in any narrow order, and bearing the cross? . . . What power of holy oil for the divine call or for ordination? Are they rich in treasures, or do they form a separate people with language, king and high priests? They are cut off from us, as the Georgians are from us and some from yourselves . . . ".[27]

The T'ondrakec'i movement was not simply religious dissension but a movement that raised deeper issues with respect to the interrelation of social, political factors. Religious developments played an important role in shaping Armenia's attitude towards its powerful neighbours. Byzantine annexation espoused separatism with regard to the empire, which was largely an ethnic, social and cultural separatism that expressed itself in religious terms. The hidden revulsion created by the rather cavalier attempts to enforce religious conformity expressed itself through various heterodox movements such as Paulicianism, Iconoclasm and T'ondrakianism.

The fact that the leader of the T'ondrakec'is, Smbat of Zarehawan, was executed by the Arab emir Aplvard, and that Grigor Magistros took extreme measures to suppress the movement indicate that it was more than just Christian religious dissent. In all the sources there is ample evidence which shows that the T'ondrakec'i movement was not static or governed by rigid dogmatic principles. In the less stable and more turbulent period of the expanding cities, when traditional bonds between men and their rural communities were being loosened, and new economic and political bonds were being created (the conquest of Ani in 1045 by Byzantium), the T'ondrakec'i sect had a natural appeal, for it bound together men of similar ideals. In Armenia they found the widest support.

We find explicit evidence of this gradual development and growing strength in the letters of Grigor Magistros. He writes: "The column raised by the Manichaeans, that is the T'ondrakec'is, has been overthrown by my humble agency . . . and that after these people had for more than two hundred years infested the whole land, and raised up the fire-altar of their lust and lewdness, and all the time Christ's flock was neglected by pastors and heads of pastors, by kings and princes, and wellnigh by all men".[28] On another occasion Grigor writes: "When I reached Mesopotamia, I rooted out of the land the tares sown by them. But then seeing how the fouling of the water increased, I followed the stream to the source, and came to the fire altar of T'ondrak".[29] He stresses the same point in another context as well: "And I came to Mesopotamia and encountered the deadly, stormy, muddy flood which, flowing forth from the cursed T'ondrakec'i Smbat, rolled death along in its waves".[30]

It is established that Mesopotamia, which extended south of Erznka from Ani to the lake of Covk', was, prior to 1045, the border land between Armenia and the Byzantine empire. This proves that the T'ondrakec'is were also active in these very critical areas.[31] Grigor Magistros, when describing his actions against the sect, relates that he had found a number of letters sent from all parts of Armenia to the T'ondrakec'i leader Yesu. This particular detail is very interesting for it sheds some light on the organisation of the sect and its nature and extent of operations. "Those priests who came forward and made known their heresies, and who were first baptized and took the names of Polycarp and Nicanor, informed us that the letters which had come from various districts to the godless leader Yesu, were to be found in those hovels of lewdness. Make haste, they said, seize and read them, and you will find in them the perversities of these devilishly minded men. Well, we looked for them, found and read them; and they were full of wicked magic and lewdness; and this among other things has been made a ground of complaint against us".[32]

This testimony shows that the movement had won the support of both the lower and upper classes and had spread "to all the districts" and even more important they still kept contact with the centre and their leader. The movement may have had varied expressions in the various districts but all seem to have had the same basis for discontent and have pursued the same objectives. And it is this strong organisational quality which gave it such a formidable strength and durability for two hundred years. This bond of unity is also acknowledged by Grigor Magistros when he informs us that "I followed the stream to the source, and came to the fire-altar of T'ondrak'".[33]

As has been the case with the Paulicians, the Armenian church, with the help of Byzantium, in the eleventh century struck the final blow. Grigor Magistros, the chief persecutor of the sect, writes: "We ordered their roof-trees to be thrown down and burned, and their tenants to be hunted out of our marches. To none of them, however, did we do any bodily harm, although the law prescribes that they should suffer the extreme penalty. And, prior to ourselves, many generals and magistrates have given them over to the sword, and, without pity have spared neither old men nor children; and quite rightly. What is more, our patriarchs have branded their foreheads and burned into them the image of a fox; others again have put their eyes out. 'You are blind' they said, 'to spiritual things; therefore you shall not look on sensible things'."[34]

Heresy was an easy word to bandy about and sometimes a convenient stick with which to beat one's enemies. The word could denote more than erroneous theology and many tensions in medieval life gave rise to controversies in which charges of heresy were loosely made. Men could speak of "heresy" when they meant schism, resistance within the church to administration, political opposition, intellectual arrogance. The concord that existed between the ecclesiastical and secular powers saw heresy as being a danger to both. It was the confrontation of the ideal of one man's mind with the existing reality that released revolutionary action into the world of Christendom. The intolerance of the Armenian church towards the T'ondrakec'i movement and the intimate involvement of church and state in its suppression indicate that:

The movement persisted for two centuries because the theological concern of the sect was not divided from the social. The evils of the age were attributable to the contemporary lapse of Christian standards. The Church must lead the way by reforming itself and setting the example of practical Christianity by sacrificing much of its wealth, relieving the monasteries of their excess of this world's goods. The grounds for doctrinal dissension and their interaction on social and economic developments provided fertile soil for the acceptance and spread of the practices of the T'ondrakec'is.

The T'ondrakec'i movement would not have been so fiercely attacked and persecuted had it not developed into a popular movement that drew far-reaching social and political conclusions from its religious convictions. Obviously the movement did make certain social and political demands and as a result found considerable support. The movement spread over the entire country causing serious disturbances. It was in some measure a popular uprising of the peasantry and the poorer classes of the towns against the feudal lords and the wealthy hierarchy. And it is these implications that forced the Armenian, Arab and Byzantine authorities jointly to condemn the sect and assist each other in its suppression.

Aristakēs Lastiverc'i says: "For it is easy to be on one's guard against outside enemies, but it is hard to shelter oneself from the assaults of one's own kinsmen, as happened to Abeła and Joseph. Now these enemies of ours, had they been of foreign speaking races, no matter one could easily be guarded against; but as the blessed John writes: 'They went out from us, but they were not of us' and therefore it is difficult to know them".[35]

Grigor of Narek calls the executor of Smbat of Zarehawan "a rod of anger in the hand of the Lord Jesus";[36] while Grigor Magistros requests those sectarians who had survived the persecution to "leave us and our land in Mesopotamia, and all who are under the supremacy of the holy kingdom of the Romans [Byzantines], in peace and quiet; teach and confirm your evil heresy neither by writing nor by speech. And now may their blood and your own be on your head".[37]

The presence of the T'ondrakec'is in Syrian Mesopotamia is also very interesting. Grigor Magistros in his letter to the Syrian patriarch requests that the latter should also denounce the heretics and since "God has made thee worthy of the struggle and campaign, in order that thou, like the other fathers, thy predecessors, mightest take the field against the God-resisting sword of heretical wizardry and against the mischievous gabble of this obscure race".[38]

These quotations are enough to prove that the T'ondrakec'i movement was closely associated with political events and circumstances. The movement was opposed to both the internal and the external enemies of Armenian society.

Appendix I

FEUDALISM IN ARMENIA

This institution was studied by Professor Adontz in his first great work,*Armenia in the period of Justinian: The political conditions based on the naxarar system*, translated by N. G. Garsoian (Lisbon, 1970), Chapter XV, pp.327-371.

The validity of Adontz's thesis of a similarity between the Armenian *naxarar* system and western feudalism rests entirely on the premise that the term "feudalism" may properly be applied to other than medieval-European institutions. This thesis of similarity between the Armenian *naxarar* system and west-European feudalism has found favour among many Soviet scholars.

The whole section on feudalism should be reviewed in the light of the more recent studies of this institution, which have dated some of Adontz's concepts. The interpretation of feudalism and the understanding of the term have developed extensively since the beginning of the century, and the problems have been complicated by the disagreement of western and Marxist scholars on some of the fundamental aspects. The most important work to be consulted is of necessity C. Toumanoff's, *Studies in Christian Caucasian History* (Washington, D.C., 1963), pp.33-144, in which he elaborates the crucial distinction between Armenian feudalism and dynasticism (p.110). There are important dissimilarities observed by Toumanoff, derived from the general survival of what is called "dynasticism" in the "feudal" pattern such as the apparent absence of the crucial act of homage as distinct from the oath of fealty (p.117, n.192). Without this distinction, the question of the correctness with which the Armenian *naxarar* system may be called "feudal" in the western sense cannot receive a valid answer. On the question of the extension of the term "feudalism" to various institutions, see R. Coulborn (ed.), *Feudalism in History* (Princeton, 1956), which is, however, poor on Armenia. The entire question of comparison must evidently hinge on the crucial and debated definition of the term "feudalism" and the legitimacy of applying it to non-European societies.

A general survey, with excellent bibliographies and discussion, on feudalism in the Byzantine Empire is provided by G. Ostrogorsky, "Agrarian conditions in the Byzantine Empire in the Middle Ages" in: *Cambridge Economic History of Europe, I* (1942), pp.194-223; 579-583; A. A. Vasiliev, "On the question of Byzantine Feudalism", *B,* VIII (1933), pp.584-603; E. H. Kantorowicz, "Feudalism in the Byzantine Empire", pp.151-166 in: *Feudalism in History*, edited by R. Coulborn; P. Charanis,

Social, Economic and Political Life in the Byzantine Empire, Collected Studies (London, 1973), pp.53-118, 39-57, 94-153, 412-24.

Appendix II

THE PHUNDAGIAGITAE

Was there a relation between the T'ondrakec'i and the Phundagiagitae sects?

The earliest document concerning the Phundagiagitae is a letter by a certain Byzantine monk Euthymius, addressed to his compatriots of the diocese of Acmonia in the province of Phrygia in Asia Minor.[1] This letter (A.D.1050), associates the sect with the T'ondrakec'is and ascribes an Armenian origin to them. Some scholars have accepted this identification (G. Ficker, K. Ter Mkrttschian, N. Akinian) and have suggested that the name should be interpreted as *T'ondragiagites.*

The name Phundagiagitae has not yet received a satisfactory explanation. On the one hand the name Phundagiagitae/Phundaitae is derived from "φοῦδαι" itself a Greek form of the Latin *phunda* meaning a bag or scrip that the heretics were supposed to have carried. The heretics are supposed to have acquired this name from their life of poverty, which compelled them to beg for their living.[2] On the other hand, some other scholars have associated the name with the supposed founder of the sect, a certain Phoundas, a disciple of Mani. According to Akinian, as in the Slavic languages, so also in the Greek of the tenth and eleventh centuries the Armenian sound "*t*" (թ) could also have been translated with the Greek "φ" (ph), cf. Russian Aphanasia= Athanasia.[3]

According to Euthymius of Acmonia's *Letter,*[4] John Tzurillas was the first teacher of this "newly appeared heresy". Euthymius accuses John of unlawfully assuming the monastic garb, forcing his wife to enter a nunnery and living unchastely.[5]

According to Euthymius, the heretics rejected the Christian dogmas of the Resurrection of the Dead, of the Second Coming, and of the Last Judgment. They rejected the Old Testament, the order of the priesthood and the worship of saints, saying "God alone is holy"; all the prayers of the Church, with the exception of the Lord's Prayer, they described as "babbling" or "vain repetitions" (cf. Matt. VI: 7), and they denied the efficacy of the Cross, the validity of Baptism and of the Eucharist.[6] The Phundagiagitae used the New Testament for exegetical purpose and relied above all on the Gospels and the Acts of the Apostles. Euthymius also mentions the Epistles of Paul as an object of their particular veneration. The Phundagiagitae apparently claimed that the words of the Gospels and of St. Paul "breathed again" owing to their interpretation of them. One of their basic quotations and sources of doctrine was St. Paul's statement "for whatever does not proceed from faith is sin" (*Romans,* 14: 23). According to Euthymius they called themselves Christians.

Thus the movement with its teachings and claims bears a very close resemblance to that of the Armenian T'ondrakec'is, if not identical. As with the Paulicians and the T'ondrakec'is, so also the main concern of the Phundagiagitae seems to have been to emphasise the spiritual dimension of Christianity, at the same time taking care to avoid confrontation with the orthodox. Euthymius identifies the Phundagiagitae with the Bogomils[7] and there is no reason to doubt this judgment.

Appendix III

NEW EVIDENCE ON YOVHANNĒS THE PRIEST: AUTHOR OF *THE KEY OF TRUTH*[1]

In a letter dated 1791 the Armenian kat'ołikos Łukas informs the Armenian patriarch of Constantinople of a certain individual whom he has put in prison at Ējmiacin for having denounced his faith several times and, more significantly, that while in Karin and in Xnus "he has associated himself with the T'ondrakec'i evil sect". From the subsequent correspondence of the kat'ołikos it becomes apparent that Yovhannēs, the sectarian, after being imprisoned in Ējmiacin for six months, managed to escape to Xnus. There is enough information about the events that followed to be able to reconstruct the history of his final arrest and tragic death.

Who was this mysterious character accused of having affiliation with the T'ondrakec'i sect? Before attempting to answer this question, we must describe in some detail a chain of events that occurred about half a century later and the debates that followed. The study of these events will facilitate the task of answering the above question.

In 1837 the Armenian bishop at Karin directed the attention of the Armenian ecclesiastical authorities to the appearance in the village of Ark'weli in Russian Armenia of a group of heretics who had migrated from the Armenian provinces dominated by the Turks, at the close of the Russo-Turkish War of 1828-1829. Upon this the Synod of the Armenian church began an investigation into the tenets and practices of the sectarians. Two priests were despatched to the village of Ark'weli to make the investigation. All the confessions were negative. The people reluctantly confessed that they had known the priest in Xnus, who had taught the heresy in question, but declared that they had not only refused to receive him, but had "anathematized him".[2] Finally, they gave a written promise "forever to repudiate the evil heresy and to remain steadfast in the confession and the laws of the orthodox Armenian church".

The Synod sent a request to the military governor of the Caucasus "to direct the local civil authorities to watch the conduct and activities of the inhabitants of Ark'weli with an eye to the heresy which had appeared in their midst". As to the nature of the heresy in question, the Synod wrote: "The heresy of the T'ondrakec'is consists in this, that they reject the mediation of saints, contemn their images, deny the use of fasts, repudiate the value of prayers, reject the immaculateness of the Holy Virgin Mother of God and the sacrament of Baptism".

This correspondence between the Synod and the civil authorities was still in progress when, in December 1837, an advice came to the Synod from the spiritual authorities of Alexandrapol (Leninakan) that a certain individual, who had only in the preceding July adopted the heresy of the T'ondrakec'is, had made an important confession: in the province of Xnus in the village of Čarum fifty-five years previously, a certain Armenian priest Ōhannēs (i.e. Yovhannēs) had joined the sect, and composed a book called *The Key of Truth*. This Ōhannēs, under pressure from the Ottoman government, had afterwards, along with his companions and family, accepted the Mohammedan faith.[3]

In the meantime, the civil and criminal court of Tiflis, having investigated the whole case from 1837 to 1845, had declared that the sectarians, under the criminal laws of 1842, were subject to be drafted into the army; but inasmuch as they had organised their sect before the promulgation of the amnesty of 1841, the court, pursuant to the first article of that amnesty, had first decided only to demand the cost of each heretic's trial; but later they were exiled to Siberia.[4]

This disclosure led to the seizure of a manuscript entitled *The Key of Truth* now preserved in the Armenian Matenadaran under no.6710. It is written on octavo paper in minuscule and consists of about 149 pages. The work, which is purely dogmatic in nature, contains some seventeen chapters of explanation and admonition on the faith, stressing in particular the significance and the importance of baptism. This section is followed by an account of the ritual to be used for baptism and ordination, some additional chapters of commentary on various minor points, and a catechism. The sole copy of the text is mutilated. About thirty-eight pages were destroyed before its surrender, and numerous words have been carefully and deliberately erased. Furthermore, the existing manuscript is not the original version of the treatise, but a copy made in the province of Tarōn in 1782.

The relationship of the sectarians to the book *The Key of Truth* became a subject for debate in academic circles. After the fourteenth century, the Armenian sources ceased to speak of the T'ondrakec'is and now suddenly a curious document attested the survival of the T'ondrakec'is, in the very same historical environment. Besides this external association the sectarians had preserved and transferred from Xnus to Širak the manual of their teachings in the shape of the book *The Key of Truth*. One important consideration to bear in mind is that we do not possess any Paulician or T'ondrakec'i writings. The ferocious persecution to which they were subjected had long since obliterated all the records of their activities, and all that was known concerning their concepts, beliefs and activities derived from their opponents.

The attention of scholars was first called to *The Key of Truth* and its contents by Alexander Eric'ian in 1880. In the *P'orj* for October he described in detail the whole movement of Xnus, the investigation that followed, and published extracts from *The Key of Truth* – and made the following observation in his conclusion "It would be very difficult to identify the sect of 1837 with the T'ondrakec'is, had not the above manual *The Key of Truth* been discovered in the possession of the Ark'weli inhabitants". While discussing the possible affiliation of the ancient and modern T'ondrakec'is he reminds us that "sectarian movements do not cease to exist but usually after periods of inactivity re-emerge having undergone various changes".[5]

The next scholar to study the subject was Sargisean in 1893[6], who was convinced that, apart from the similarity of names, there is nothing in common between the ancient and modern T'ondrakec'is and that *The Key of Truth* could not have been written before 1782. Therefore we can do no more than conclude on the basis of internal evidence that the doctrines of *The Key of Truth* are a synthesis of Manichaean, Calvinist and Lutheran doctrines, and consequently the above sectarians were not T'ondrakec'is but Neo-Manichaeans, Calvinists or Lutherans.

The above two studies and the findings of the Synod prompted K. Ter Mkrttschian to write an article in the *Zeitschrift für Kirchengeschichte.*[7] The article contains an abridged translation of *The Key of Truth.* The author is of the opinion that the document reveals explicit Anabaptist influence, and in this connection quotes from the archives of the Synod an incident which shows how the sectarians performed the two most important sacraments of the Church: Baptism and Communion. Their baptism had been administered in connection with the Lord's Supper, wherein the elements used had been a loaf of plain unleavened bread, and wine served in a common vessel placed on a wooden table. Upon the bread they pronounced the words: "Take eat this is the body of our Lord Jesus Christ". Upon the wine, the words: "This is the blood of our Lord Jesus Christ". The candidate for baptism had approached the table uncovered, when the ministering officer had poured upon his head a handful of water, saying: "In the name of the Father", then a second handful, saying: "And of the Son" then a third, saying: "And of the Holy Spirit, Amen". From this Ter Mkrttschian supposes that the author of *The Key of Truth* had been to Europe and while there had associated with some Anabaptists from whom he had picked up these tenets and practices. He continues "unfortunately it is still a mystery, as to whether *The Key of Truth* is altogether a new creation of Ōhannēs, or is composed of various ancient documents, or is just a copy of an old treatise".

But on finding some Gnostic elements in the document he concludes that these sectarians could well have been the remnants of the ancient T'ondrakec'is, who for centuries had been loyal to their principles and practices and under the influence of the new Protestant activities were once again revitalised.

In 1898 Conybeare[8] published the text of *The Key of Truth* with the English translation. Despite the lateness of the surviving document, Conybeare, accepted *The Key of Truth* as an authentic work originally composed in the period between the seventh and the ninth centuries, while he believed the prayers and the sections related to the Liturgy to be "older than the controversial chapters which accompany them, and to belong to the fourth or fifth century".[9] Conybeare regarded Smbat of Zarehawan, the T'ondrakec'i leader, as the author of *The Key of Truth* and wrongly identified him with the Bagratid Smbat the Confessor.[10] He insisted that the doctrines of *The Key of Truth* were similar to those doctrines preached by the Monarchianists of the second century.

Garsoian, in spite of accepting the fact that the "script is not the original version of the treatise, but a copy made in the province of Tarōn in 1782"[11], agrees with Conybeare that the archaic language of the text indicates that the work itself may have been composed as early as the ninth century. Garsoian writes that the obvious possibility of alteration of vocabulary and style in the course of many copyings makes the linguistic evidence for dating the original composition of *The Key of Truth* at best inconclusive. But on the evidence of theological similarity between the doctrine of *The Key of Truth* and that found in the medieval sources, *The Key of Truth* is an authentic work originally composed in the period between the seventh and ninth centuries.[12] This is remarkable, but not surprising, for Garsoian sees the T'ondrakec'i sect as a continuation of Paulicianism. But as I have endeavoured to show, the T'ondrakec'i movement in Armenia began independently of the Paulicians.

Conybeare's demonstration that the language, style and doctrines of *The Key of Truth* are most closely related to those of Armenian authors of the ninth and tenth centuries has been questioned by critics and all scholars who have in some form or other written about *The Key of Truth*. The main opposition to the ninth-century date assigned to the treatise by Conybeare came from Macler[13]: "Je crois que M. Conybeare s'est un peu avancé en datant *La Clef de la Vérité* du IXe siècle. L'imprécision même du style porterait à faire descendre beaucoup plus bas la date de rédaction de ce précieux document des Pauliciens". This opinion is also shared by Meillet[14]: "M. Conybeare fait remonter la composition jusqu'au milieu du IXe siècle. Sans vouloir diminuer la très haute importance de la publication, il sera permis d'exprimer des doutes à ce sujet . . . les probabilités sont pour une époque plus récente". The English reviewer wrote "in this obscure and persecuted sect we are told to recognise the sole survivor of primitive, ante-Nicene Christianity . . . This is a tremendous claim and needs to be proved up to the hilt. His book suffers from a too enthusiastic appreciation of *The Key*".[15] The German reviewer Bonwetsch[16] regarded the thesis of Conybeare as unconvincing and observed that there is no relation between *The Key of Truth* and Smbat of Zarehawan or with the T'ondrakec'i sect in general.

We said earlier that Conybeare accepted *The Key of Truth* as a work originally composed in the period between the seventh and ninth centuries. As final evidence for the above conclusion Conybeare quotes a passage from the colophon: "I humbly entreat you with warm love and faith to forgive the shortcomings and the insufficiencies: they are not due to ourselves, but have found their way into it as being of unpractised copyists". This is an indication, Conybeare observes, that the work "before it reached his hands in 1782, had been handed down through several generations" and therefore the remark is the copyist's. But in my opinion the above observation was made by the author himself, and it makes no sense if attributed to the alleged copyist. If we take full account of the whole colophon in which the author speaks about his undertaking in terms and in a style very similar to the exordium, it convinces us that both are from the same pen. Conybeare accepts the exordium as being "unmistakably from the pen of some great leader and missionary of the Paulician church".[17]

The reason behind this inconsistency is that many scholars think that because the word "all-glorious" (amenapaycaṙ) is written in small letters, it may be an incomplete word and the continuation of a sentence. But from the manuscript we get no impression of pages missing at this point, and therefore the colophon is also by the author Yovhannēs Vahaguni. There could be several explanations for the colophon. It may be that Yovhannēs Vahaguni dictated the work to a copyist and then deleted the errors; or that after having seen the various copies of his work, he added the above colophon to his manuscript; or simply that, being incapable of writing correctly himself, he blamed potential future copyists.

Conybeare's demonstration that the language and style of *The Key* are most closely related to those of Armenian authors of the ninth and tenth centuries is inconclusive. It is true that *The Key of Truth* is written in the classical form of Armenian. The sixth century is considered as the line of demarcation between the use of classical Armenian and the vulgar tongue which rapidly predominated,[18] so the fact that classical Armenian was a dead language by the tenth century is not a strong argument for assigning the composition of *The Key* to a period not later than the tenth century. Abełyan[19] has shown the occasional archaising use of classical Armenian as late as the nineteenth century. This is particularly true of ecclesiastical writers. One must not forget that the author of the document, Yovhannēs Vahaguni, had been to the monastery at Venice and it is very difficult to estimate accurately his knowledge of classical Armenian, particularly since the sections on prayer, liturgy and scriptures (in which Conybeare sees a clear style) contain verbatim quotations from corresponding religious literature. So that to regard the work as belonging to the eighth or ninth centuries on the basis of language and style is not possible.

What do we know about the author of *The Key of Truth*? The Ark'weli deacon Gevork' Sargisian from whom in 1838 the document was seized by the Armenian ecclesiastical authorities, had prior to that destroyed a number of pages, particularly from the colophon, where we would expect to find information about the author. Fortunately we have important evidence about the author and his manual and how it reached Ark'weli, in a written recantation dated 20th January 1838, by the same Gevork' Sargisian and signed by twelve Ark'weli residents. The text is as follows:

> We the undersigned, inhabitants of Ark'weli, submit this religious document to the authorities at Gumri to the effect that during the Ottoman occupation, there appeared in the village of Čarum a priest named Ōhannēs, who had narrated a book called *The Key of Truth*, who himself became a Muslim and died tragically. While he was alive he gave this book to Mesrop Budałian and Mesrop gave it to Kirakos Avdalian when he migrated. After the death of Kirakos the book was in

> the possession of his son, who with the deacon Gevorkʻ Sargisian had read the book and had believed in everything that was written in it, regarding it an authentic scripture, which they also taught to Sargis . . . But now, knowing that everything written in the book is false and anti-Christian and against the beliefs of the Armenian Church, we repent and seek forgiveness . . . [20]

This evidence of the Arkʻweli residents and other indirect sources leaves us in no doubt that this Ōhannēs and the Yovhannēs mentioned in the letters of the katʻołikos quoted at the beginning of this chapter are one and the same person.

The first reference to Ōhannēs in the letters of the katʻołikos Łukas dates back to 13th July 1789. In this letter the katʻołikos enquires about a "certain priest who is in Xnus".[21] Therefore, the ecclesiastical authorities in Ēǰmiacin knew about the sectarian movement as early as 1789 but had taken no steps against it. In his biography Paul Meherian[22] writes that in 1773 while travelling to Karin he had met Armenians who had denounced their faith and were "such sectarians as are the Tʻondrakecʻis or Arewordikʻ".[23]

Then the account continues, that in the vicinity of Karin in the monastery of Bořčimasur a prelate by the name of Ōhannēs, assuming the style of a bishop, had ordained fourteen priests. In this connection there was great uproar and a major controversy began. In order to avoid being persecuted by the Armenians the self-styled bishop fled to Manazkert. In 1774-1781 a certain individual named Ōhannēs arrived at Constantinople, who after committing a major offence, was sentenced to eight months imprisonment. Conybeare at this point suggests that it was the Armenian patriarch who imprisoned Ōhannēs, from where the latter escaped and arrived at Xnus.[24]

Conybeare has misunderstood Meherian, for the patriarch did not imprison Ōhannēs, but on the contrary intervened and freed Ōhannēs, from where he went to the Armenian Catholic Convent at Venice. But he did not stay there for long: for "after a few days as one demon-possessed and confused" he was banished from the Convent and returned to Constantinople. Then he married, and denied his faith and after some time travelled to Karin, then to Muš and two years later to Xnus.[25] He was ordained a priest and "Thereafter – he began to sow the seeds of his evil sect in the village of Marux and in the surrounding villages".[26]

That the above testimony of Meherian is accurate and trustworthy is clear from a letter of the katʻołikos dated 11th May 1792 and addressed to the Armenian patriarch of Constantinople, which reads: "Last year (1791) a certain priest Ōhannēs, who on several occasions has denied his faith and religion and later received ordination by force from the governor of Xnus, appeared in Karin and Xnus and is teaching his evil doctrine which is not only foul but also related to the Tʻondrakecʻis".[27] It is evident that the katʻołikos could no longer ignore or tolerate what was going on; so he took immediate steps to put an end to Ōhannēs' activities.

Soon with the help of government officials the sectarian was brought to Ēǰmiacin and imprisoned.[28] In 1791 the katʻołikos wrote to the abbot of the monastery at

Muš as follows: "I am writing to you concerning those led astray by him (Ōhannēs). Have they returned to the right path or not? Inform me about them. The one who is with us has repudiated his doctrines and seeks repentance, but I am a little apprehensive, for he may go back to his old ways. To keep him longer would not be right, for he is a family man . . . ".[29]

In 1791-1792 the abbot of the monastery at Muš wrote to the kat'ołikos regarding Ōhannēs, that the latter had repented and sought pardon. The kat'ołikos replied that, if that was so, the local inhabitants should send him a 'recommendation' guaranteeing safe conduct.

In 1792 the requested "recommendation" reached Ējmiacin. The letter which is signed by several of the priests and civil officials of Xnus, testifies that Ōhannēs had acknowledged his errors and repented.[30] But the kat'ołikos was still very cautious and extremely reluctant to free Ōhannēs. He requested two priests from Xnus and two provincials to accompany Ōhannēs to Ējmiacin "where he would be given the opportunity to demonstrate his repentance and confess personally his allegiance to the doctrines of the Armenian church, which he must promise he will never falsify, but remain always in the truth".[31]

But there is no evidence that Ōhannēs did appear before the kat'ołikos. According to Meherian, after his return the governor of Xnus, his patron, was executed in 1801, Ōhannēs was forced by the Turks to return to Islam. But this evidence is not supported. In the minutes of the Synod at Ējmiacin under 11th May 1838, it is written that the military governor of the Caucasus was informed that "one of the Armenian priests, Ōhannēs, who had fallen into this sect, has narrated a book *The Key of Truth* and when the Turks learned about the heresy of this priest, they forced him to abandon his beliefs and accept Islam with his family".[32] On 20th January 1838, the inhabitants of Ark'weli reported the death of Ōhannēs.[33]

On 28th April 1841, the inhabitants of Ark'weli under severe pressure confessed that in accordance with the teachings of *The Key of Truth* they had foolishly baptized each other, and in the register it is recorded that of those baptized, four were 60-80 years old. "Those baptized below the age of 30 are not by Ōhannēs, the follower of T'ondrakec'i, who later became a Turk (i.e. Mohammedan)."[34] In the same register we find six names, ages from thirty to fifty, who were also "baptized in the same way by a non-priest", and another was baptized by a disciple of Ōhannēs, Mesrop who died in Xnus.[35] So it is clear that in accordance with *The Key of Truth* baptism was valid only after the age of thirty and Ōhannēs had certainly adhered strictly to his own teaching. So he was still alive and active while the testimony of the inhabitants of Ark'weli suggested that he had died in western Armenia.

It seems that the Ark'welians had deliberately confused the authorities, particularly as regards chronology. This is made explicit by the text of *The Key of Truth*. On the title page of *The Key of Truth* we read that it "was copied in the era of the Saviour 1782". This has been crudely changed to 1832, while the date of the colophon 1782 was left unchanged.[36] It is difficult to say what the reason was behind these deliberate attempts at cover-up. In spite of all these confusing reports, Eric'ian, who had first-hand knowledge of the events and had investigated all the testimonies, had reached the conclusion that the author of *The Key of Truth* had been executed by the Turkish authorities.

The crucial testimony in deciding the date of Ōhannēs's death is found in a letter of the kat'ołikos Łukas to the patriarch of Constantinople dated October 1793.[37] In it the kat'ołikos writes: "to inform you about the end of the priest from Xnus, the founder of the evil sect, who fled from here, although it was reported that he had repudiated, he did not return. The governor of the place (Xnus) has executed him for his evil deeds and in this way the evil among us was removed". So Ōhannēs had been executed before October 1793.

It is very difficult to picture the role of Ōhannēs (Yovhannēs) Vahaguni in the adventurous and tempestuous life drama of the author of *The Key of Truth*. Sargisean identifies Yovhannēs Vahaguni with the self-styled bishop of Bořčimasur or the governor of Xnus, who according to him was by origin an Armenian sectarian who had later adopted the faith of Islam. This is a conjecture not yet proven. One thing is clear, namely that the execution of Yovhannēs followed the execution of his patron, the governor of Xnus. The execution of the latter may have been due to his sympathies towards the sectarians or because he did not take appropriate action against the sect.

The conclusion from this discussion is that *The Key of Truth* is a corrupted document, owing to later additions, and therefore it is not possible to form from it an opinion about the ancient T'ondrakec'i movement.

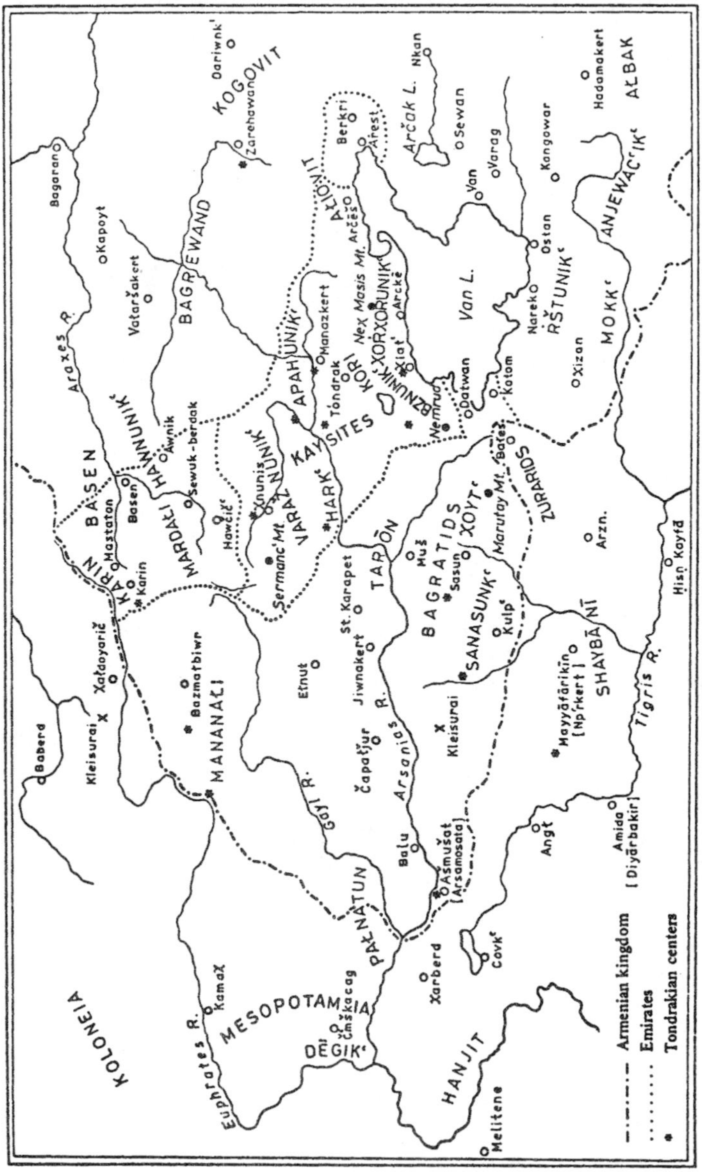
KOLONEIA
Euphrates R.
Kamax
MESOPOTAMIA
DEGIK'
PAŁNATUN
HANJIT
Melitene
Xarberd
Covk'
Balu
Arsanias R.
Gayl R.
MANANAŁI
Bazmatbiwr
Kleisurai
Babera
Xałdoyarič
KARIN
Karin
Mastaton
BASEN
Basen
HAMNUNIK'
MARDAŁI
Hawčič'
Sewuk-berdak
Awnik
Araxes R.
Vataršakert
Kapoyt
Bagaran
BAGREWAND
KOGOVIT
Zarehawan
Dariwnk'
AŁIOVIT
Berkri
Arčēš
Arest
Arčak L.
Nkan
Sewan
Varag
Van
Kangowar
Hadamakert
AŁBAK
ANJEWAC'IK'
MOKK'
ŘŠTUNIK'
Ostan
Nareko
Xizan
Van L.
Arckē
Nex Masis Mt.
XORXORUNIK'
Manazkert
APAHUNIK'
Tondrak
KORI
KAYSITES
Xlat'
BZNUNIK'
Nemrud
Datwan
Kotom
Bałēš
ZURARIDS
XOYT'
Marutay Mt.
HARK'
VARAŻNUNIK'
Xnunis
Sermanc' Mt.
TARŌN
Muš
St. Karapet
Etnut
Jiwnakert
Čapałjur
BAGRATIDS
Sasun
SANASUNK'
Kulp'
Arzn.
Hisn Kayfā
Tigris R.
SHAYBĀNĪ
Mayyāfārikīn
[Np'rkert]
Amida
[Diyārbakir]
Angł
Asmušat
[Arsamosata]
Armenian kingdom
Emirates
Tondrakian centers

NOTES TO CHAPTER II
(pp. 7 - 24)

1. *Movsēs Xorenac'i,* ***History of the Armenians.*** *Translation and commentary on the literary sources by Robert W. Thomson (Harvard University Press, 1978), p.330.*
2. *Koriwn,* ***Vark' Maštoc'i,*** *M. Abeɫyan, ed. (Erevan, 1941), p.68.*
3. *Ibid., p.40.*
4. *Movsēs Xorenac'i,* ***History of the Armenians,*** *p.331.*
5. *H. G. Melk'onyan,* ***Hay-asorakan haraberut'yunneri patmut'yunic'*** *(From the history of Armenian-Syrian relations) (Erevan, 1970), pp.67-70.*
6. ***Kanonagirk' Hayoc'*** *(Book of Armenian canons), A. Ɫlčean, ed. (Tiflis, 1913), pp. 80-82. English translation from N. Garsoian,* ***The Paulician Heresy*** *(The Hague, 1967), pp.82-83.*
7. *St. T. Melik'-Baxšyan,* ***Pavɫikyan šaržumê Hayastanum*** *(The Paulician movement in Armenia) (Erevan, 1953), pp.76-77.*
8. ***Kanonagirk' Hayoc',*** *Vazgen Hakobyan, ed. (Erevan, 1964), pp.534-535.*
9. *Aristakēs Lastiverc'i,* ***History,*** *K. N. Yuzbašyan, ed.(Erevan, 1963), xxiii, p.133.*
10. *Matenadaran, MS.795, fol.129a.*
11. *Georgius Monachus,* ***Chronicon,*** *C. de Boor, ed.(Leipzig, 1904), p.721.*
12. *Petrus Siculus,* ***Historia,*** *PG, CIV, 1253.*
13. *Grigor Magistros,* ***Letters,*** *p.16; H. M. Bartikyan, 'Otvetnoe poslanie Grigoruya Pakhlavuni Siriyskomu katolikosu' (The answer of Grigor Pahlavouni to the Catholicos of Syria),* ***Palestinskiy Sbornik,*** *7(70)(1962), p.139.*
14. *K. N. Yuzbašyan, 'K istorii Pavlikianskogo dvizheniia v Vizantii v IX vv',* ***Voprosy istorii religii i ateizma,*** *IV (Moscow, 1956), pp.246-279.*
15. *Occurs in the text of the canons of the Council of Dvin (554) in the "Oath of Union",* ***BL*** *(Tiflis, 1901), p.73. In the text the name appears in the genitive form:* ***Pawɫikeanac',*** *which is also the form used by Yovhannēs Ōjnec'i (717-728) in the discourse 'Contra Paulicianos'; see* ***Domini Johannis Philosophi Ozniensis armenorum catholici opera,*** *par R. P. Johannem Bapt. Aucher (Venice, 1834), p.78.*
16. *Occurs in the Canons of the Council of Albania in 702-705, Samuēl of Ani,* ***Collection from Historical Writings,*** *p.286. The genitive form would be* ***Paylikeanc'.*** *The correct explanation of this form was first given by H. M. Bart'ikyan*

in 'Pavlikyan šaržman mi k'ani albyurneri gnahatman surǰē' (Concerning the evaluation of certain sources on the Paulician movement)(Erevan, 1961), pp. 31-33 and in 'Armyanskie istochniki dlya izucheniya istorii Pavlikianskogo dvizheniya' (Armenian sources for the study of the Paulician movement), ***Palestinskiy Sbornik****, 4(67)(1959), pp.133-146. It is in the nominative case and is used in this form in the Canons of the Council of Dvin in 719.* ***Kanonagirk' Hayoc'****, p.516. This form is also used by Dawit' son of Alavka,* ***paylikeank'-n****, see M. Baxšyan,* ***Pavlikyan šaržumě Hayastanum****, p.135.*

17. *Grigor Magistros,* ***Letters****, p.161. Derives from the form* ***Pawlikeank'****.*

18. *In the Canons of the Council of Dvin,* ***Kanonagirk' Hayoc'****, p.516, see note 8 for the variants of this form of the name.*

19. *Occurs in the Canons of the Council of Dvin,* ***ibid****., p.516.*

20. *In the Canons of the Council of Dvin,* ***ibid****., pp.516-8,* ***Pōlikeank'*** *is the variant form of* ***Pawlikeank'****.*

21. *See Canon XXXII, p.534. In the variant forms there is also the form* ***molikeank'****. This is another interpretation of the word. 'moli' means 'possessive'. The form* ***Polikeank'*** *occurs in the works of Grigor of Narek, Matenadaran MS. 1568; cf. K. Yuzbašyan, 'Tondrakskoe dvizhenie v Armenii i Pavlikiane' (The T'ondrakian movement in Armenia and the Paulicians),* ***IANA****, 9 (1956), p.34.*

22. *K. Ter Mkrttschian,* ***Die Paulikianer****, p.63. This explanation has been widely accepted. See F. C. Conybeare,* ***The Key of Truth****, p.cv; S. Runciman,* ***The Medieval Manichee****, p.47; M. Loos, 'Deux contributions à l'histoire des Pauliciens', and 'Origine du nom des Pauliciens',* ***BS****, XVIII (1957), p.213; N. Garsoian,* ***The Paulician Heresy****, p.145; E. G. Ter Minasyan,* ***Miǰnadaryan alandneri cagman ev zargac'man patmut'yunic'*** *(History of the rise and development of sects in the Middle Ages)(Erevan, 1968), p.117.*

23. *H. Bart'ikyan,* ***Sources****, p.108, n.8.*

24. *The identification is tempting especially since Hübschmann and Ačaryan trace* ***mclnē*** *back to the Syriac* ***mêṣallêyānē****, whence the name Messalians is derived.*

25 *H. Ačaryan,* ***Etymological dictionary of the Armenian language*** *(Erevan, 1931) Vol. V, pp.818-819.*

26. *M. Abelyan,* ***History of Armenian Literature****, pp.620-7.*

27. *H. Bart'ikyan,* ***Sources****, p.36, n.3; K. N. Yuzbašyan, 'De l'origine du nom «Pauliciens»',* ***REA****, IX (1972), pp.355-77.*

28. *Mas'ūdī,* ***Le livre de l'avertissement et de la revision****,* ***BGA****, VIII, p.151; 163; Qudāma,* ***Kitāb a-kharādj****.* ***BGA****, V, p.254. See Hewsen, 'Armenia according to the Ašxarahac'uyc'.* ***REA****, II (1965), p.333, n.60. Paytakaran is the flatland between the Kur and Arax rivers including the plain of Mughan south of the*

latter. It may even have stretched to the Caspian Sea, and included the Apcheron Peninsula. Its chief city bore the same name and was called Baylakan by the Arab writers. In the ninth century large numbers of Paulicians fleeing from the hostilities of the Byzantine officials took refuge in Baylakan under Arab protection.

29. *N. Garsoian,* **The Paulician Heresy**, *pp.13-17.*

30. **PG**. *CIV, 1280.*

31. **Ibid.**, *1285.*

32. **Ibid.**, *1297.*

33. *Georgius Monachus,* **Chronicon**, *II, pp.718-719.*

34. *Arsamosata: H. Grégoire, 'Précisions géographiques et chronologiques sur les Pauliciens',* **ARB-BL**, *5e série XXXIII (1947), p.289: M. Loos, 'Le mouvement Paulicien à Byzance'* **BS**, *XXIV (1903), pp.259-60; Hewsen, 'Armenia according to the Ašxarhac'uyc',* **REA**, *II (1965), p.327 n.21. Balahovit is the other name for Arsamosata. The canton is the classical Bolbene or Balabitene. In Latin it is known as Arsamosata; G. Huxley, 'The historical geography of the Paulician and T'ondrakian heresies',* **Medieval Armenian Culture**, *ed. by Thomas J. Samuelian (Scholars Press, 1982), pp.81-95.*

35. **PG**, *CIV, 1273.*

36. *Photius, 'Contra Manichaeos',* **PG**, *CII, 16-17. H. Bart'ikyan,* **Sources**, *p.169.*

37. **PG**, *CIV, 1283-84.*

38. **PG**, *CII, 52. The suggestion put forward by Garsoian in* **Paulician Heresy**, *pp.198-203, that the Paulicians were branded 'Manichaean' because their iconoclastic tendencies connected them with the Byzantine iconoclasts, who were, in turn, according to the iconophile, Manichaean despisers of matter, is quite unconvincing. 'Manichaean', like 'Jew' and 'pagan', was simply a standard and indiscriminate term of abuse. The related suggestion that an extreme docetic iconoclasm formed the middle term of transition between the early adoptionist Christology of the early Paulicians, and a later dualistic aberrant mysticism, is also quite undemonstrable; in particular it operates with a notion of 'docetic iconoclasm' which is an invention of iconophile polemicists.*

39. *F. C. Conybeare,* **The Key of Truth**, *p.cv; S. Runciman,* **The Medieval Manichee**, *pp.48-49.*

40. *H. Bart'ikyan,* **Sources**, *p.28.*

41. *Theodore Balsamon, Canones Conciliorum,* **PG**, *CXXXVII, see H. Bart'ikyan,* **Sources**, *pp.28-29.*

42. *N. Garsoian, **The Paulician Heresy**, pp.211-12; F. C. Conybeare, **op.cit.**, p.cvi.*

43. *This association was emphasised by F. Scheidweiler, 'Paulikianerprobleme'. **BZ**, XLIII, (1950), pp.366-72.*

44. *N. Garsoian, **The Paulician Heresy**, pp.212 ff; Cf. **REA**, I (1964), p.454.*

45. *H. Bart'ikyan, **op. cit.**, p.139, n.3.*

46. ***PG**, CIV, 1245.*

47. *Mas'ūdī, **Le Livre de l'avertissement**, p.208.*

48. *K. N. Yuzbašyan, 'Tondrakskoe dvizhenie', p.38, n.57*

49. *Georgius Monachus, **Chronicon**, II, p.720.*

50. *D. Obolensky, **The Bogomils** (Cambridge, 1948), pp.55ff.*

51. *M. Loos, 'Deux contributions', **BS**, XVIII, 2 (1957), pp.209-12; F. Scheidweiler, 'Paulikianerprobleme', **BZ**, XLIII, 2(1950), pp.17-18; see the objections of M. Loos, 'Deux contributions', p.212, n.43.*

52. *'Sources Grecques pour l'histoire des Pauliciens: Les formules d'abjuration', p.206.*

53. *G. Ficker, 'Eine Sammlung von Abschwörungsformeln', **ZKG**, XXVII (1906), pp. 453-54; M. Loos, 'Origine du nom des Pauliciens', **BS**, XVIII, 2(1957), p. 206.*

54. ***The Book of Heresies**, p.113; N. Garsoian, **The Paulician Heresy**, p.239.*

55. *Included in the **Book of Letters**, see K. Ter Mkrttschian, 'Pavłikyanc' ev T'ondrakec'voc' ałandnerê ardi K'nnadatutyamb' (The Paulician sect and the T'ondrakec'i in the light of contemporary criticism), **Ararat** (July, 1900), pp.328-333; N. Garsoian, **The Paulician Heresy**, pp.236-7.*

56. *N. Garsoian, **The Paulician Heresy**. p.90.*

57. *S. Der Nersessian, 'Une apologie des images du septième siècle', **B**, XVIII (1944-45), p.71, n.55 and 86, n.131; M. Baxšyan, **Pavłikyan šaržumê Hayastanum**, p.17.*

58. *H. Bart'ikyan, **Sources**, p.88.*

59. ***Ibid.**, pp. 85-88.*

60. *E. G. Ter Minasyan, **Mijnadaryan ałandneri**, p.141.*

61. *See English transl. in N. Garsoian, **The Paulician Heresy**, p.89.*

62. ***Kanonagirk' Hayoc'**, A. Łlčean, ed. (Tiflis, 1914), pp.164-73.*

63. ***Kanonagirk' Hayoc'**, pp.187, 195, 235, 383-84, 385, 399-400, 486.*

64. *K. N.Yuzbašyan, 'K istorii Pavlikianskogo', p.272.*

65. ***Kanonagirk' Hayoc'**, Vol.I, p.130.*

66. *H. Bart'ikyan, **Sources**, p.111.*

67. *Movsēs Dasxuranc'i, **The history of Caucasian Albanians** (Tiflis, 1912), pp.302-305; English transl. by C. J. F. Dowsett (London, 1961), pp.171-73.*

68. *S. Der Nersessian, 'Une apologie des images du septième siècle', **B**, XVII (1944-45), pp.70-71.*

69. *S. Der Nersessian, 'Image worship in Armenia and its opponents', **Armenian Quarterly**, 1, (1956), p.70.*

70. ***PG**, CII, 81.*

71. ***PG**, CIV, 1299-1300.*

72. ***Ibid.**, 1299-1300.*

73. ***Ibid.**, 1300b.*

74. ***Ibid.**, CII, 73.*

75. ***PG**, CII, 76.*

76. ***Ibid.**, CIV, 1299-1300.*

77. ***Ibid.**. 1300.*

78. *The 'travelling companions' of Paul are called **synekdemoi** in Acts 19:30. The Paulicians who considered themselves the true followers of Paul, not only called most of their leaders after the disciples of St. Paul, but also gave the name **synekdemoi** to their ruling body, taken from the Epistles of Paul.*

79. ***PG**, CII, 81. **Travaux et Mémoires** 4 (1970, p.67.*

80. ***PG**, CIV, 1301. There is no such word in the Greek language. Some scholars have considered it to be the interpolated form of the word μιαρός/defile, and others have understood it to mean μή ἱερεῖς/not holy, not priestly/. From the text, however, it is clear that it refers to the 'priesthood'.*

81. *The term ἄστατος in Greek means 'never standing still', 'unstable', 'inconsistent'. If we consider the above word as being Greek, then as K.Yuzbašyan has suggested we must take it to mean 'never standing still in one place' which would describe the missionaries of the Paulician sect very accurately. Ter Mkrttschian thinks that the word is not Greek. He proposed that in the term we must seek the sectarians mentioned in the Armenian sources under the name of **Cader**.*

82. ***PG**, CII, 76.*

83. ***Ibid.***, *76.*

84. *PG, CIV, 1301.*

85. *H. Bart'ikyan in* ***Istochniki dlia istoria pavlikianskogo dvizhenia*** *(Erevan, 1963), p.166, note 43, suggests that Karbeas is the Armenian name of Karapet in its diminutive form – Karpis. In the Byzantine epic* ***Digenes Akrites*** *the name occurs as Karo[es]. See H. Grégoire, 'Notes sur l'Epopée Byzantine. Une mention du héros Aukylas et du Paulicien Karbeas dans un chant akritique',* ***B***, *XIII (1938), p.251. N. G. Garsoïan, 'Byzantine Heresy',* ***DOP***, *XXV (1971), p.92, note 28, thinks Bart'ikyan's suggestion is 'quite unconvincing and farfetched'.*

86. ***PG***, *CII, 8.*

87. *G. Ficker, 'Eine Sammlung von Abschwörungsformeln',* ***ZKG***, *XXVII (1906), pp.443-464.*

88. ***PG***, *CII, 81.*

NOTES TO CHAPTER III
(pp. 25 - 36)

1. *Barhebraeus,* ***The Chronography of Gregory Abû'l Faraj . . . Bar Hebraeus,*** *E. A. W. Budge, transl. (London, 1932), p.95.*
2. *H. Manandyan,* ***Erker II*** *(Collected works), p.536.*
3. *A. Ter-Ghewondyan,* ***The Arab emirates in Bagratid Armenia,*** *p.156, n.7.*
4. *H. Nalbandyan, 'Arabneri harkayin k'ałak'akanut'yunê Hayastanum' (The taxation policy of the Arabs in Armenia), T, 12 (1956); H. Zoryan, 'Arabneri harkayin k'ałak'akanut'yunê feudalakan Hayastanum' (The taxation policy of the Arabs in feudal Armenia), T, 2-3 (1927).*
5. *R. Vasmer,* ***Chronologie der arabischen statthalter von Armenien unter den Abbasiden, von as-Saffach bis zum Krönung Aschots,*** *I (750-887); Armenian translation V. Inglizian (Vienna, 1933); W. E. Kaegi, 'al-Balādhurī and the Armeniak theme',* ***B,*** *XXXVIII (1968), p.275.*
6. *Dionysios Tell-Mahrē,* ***La Chronique de Denys de Tel-Mahré,*** *p.2.*
7. *Samuēl of Ani,* ***Collections*** *. . . p.82. In the above passage modius or griv is a unit of measurement = 9.792 kg. dirham a silver coin.*
8. *Movsēs Dasxuranc'i,* ***The History of the Caucasian Albanians,*** *C. J. F. Dowsett, ed. and trans. (London, 1961), p.209.*
9. ***Ibid.,*** *p.209, n.4.*
10. *al-Balādhurī,* ***The Book of the Conquest of Nations,*** *p.16.*
11. ***Ibid.,*** *p.10. Muhammad ibn-Marwān was governor of Armenia from 695-705.*
12. *Łewond,* ***History,*** *X, p.36.*
13. *Qudāma,* ***BGA,*** *VI, M. J. de Goeje, ed.*
14. *Łewond,* ***History,*** *XXXIII-XXXIV, pp.135-39.*
15. *Michael the Syrian,* ***History,*** *(Jerusalem, 1869), p.363*
16. *Łewond,* ***History,*** *XXXVII, p.154.*
17. *Ibn Khaldūn,* ***The Muqaddimah: an introduction to history,*** *Franz Rosenthal, trans. (London, 1958), p.364.*
18. *A. von Kremer,* ***Culturgeschichte,*** *I, p.343; J. Laurent,* ***L'arménie entre Byzance et L'islam,*** *p.203.*

19. *R. Levy,* ***Sociology of Islam****, I, p.346.*

20. ***Kitāb al Masālik Wa'l Mamālik . . . auctore Ibn Khordadhbeh****, M. J. de Goeje, ed., p.124.*

21. *Hans von Mžik, Mustafa al-Saqa (Cairo, 1938); Michael Awwad,* ***Nusus Dhaiah min Kitab al-wuzara*** *(Beirut, 1964).*
It will be noted that the receipts from the eastern provinces, where silver was plentiful, are given in silver dirhams – while Roman provinces paid in gold dinars. One dinar = 10 silver dirhams.

22. *V. Minorsky, 'Caucasica IV, The Caucasian Vassals of Marzuban in 344/955',* ***BSOAS****, XV-3 (1953), p.517.*

23. *Saint-Martin,* ***Mémoires sur L'Arménie****, p.231; cf. R. Grousset,* ***Histoire de l'Arménie****, p.451; N. Adontz,* ***Historical Studies*** *(Paris, 1948), p.143.*

24. *It is evident from the testimony of Arab and Armenian sources that the Bagratids paid the tribute not directly to the caliph but to the emir of Ādharbāydjān who in turn paid to the caliph a set sum determined for the entire tax district which included Armenia.*

25. *A. Müller,* ***History of Islam****, N. A. Mednikov, trans. (St. Petersburg, 1895), II, pp.236-237.*

26. *Yovhannēs Drasxanakertc'i,* ***History****, pp.175-176; Ibn Ḥawḳal, Kramers ed. (Leyden, 1938). On Ašot's seal it is only written 'Ašot son of Smbat' (Ashut ibn Sinbat). N. O. Laypanov, 'The seal of Ašot Bagratuni',* ***IANA****, XI (1955), pp. 97-98. [In Armenian]*

27. *Constantine Porphyrogenitus,* ***DAI****, Vol.II, Commentary pp.158-159;168-44.*

28. *Yovhannēs Drasxanakertc'i,* ***History****, p.140; R. H. Jenkins, 'Letter 101 of the Patriarch Nicolos Mysticus',* ***B****, XXI (1961), pp.75-90*

29. *Asołik,* ***Universal History****, p.161.*

30. *V. M. Harutiunyan, 'L'urbanisme en Arménie due Moyen âge',* ***REA****, n.s. V (1968), pp.51-63; H. M. Tokarckii,* ***Architektura Armenii IV-XIV VV*** *(Erevan, 1961), pp.187-89.*

31. *Yovhannēs Drasxanakertc'i,* ***History*** *pp.198-99.*

32. *Aristakēs Lastiverc'i,* ***History****, p.75.*

33. *N. Marr,* ***Ani*** *(Leningrad-Moscow, 1934).*

34. *al-Iṣṭakhrī, BGA M. J. de Goeje , ed. (Leyden, 1870), p.188.*

35. *Ibn Ḥawḳal, BGA, II, p.245;* ***Collection****, p. 92, cf. al-Muḳaddasi, BGA, III, p.377.*

36. *A. von Kremer, **Culturgeschichte des Orients**, I, p.342.*

37. *Yovhannēs Drasxanakertc'i, **History**, p.198, 210.*

38. *I. Ōrbeli, **The ruins of Ani**, p.47.*

39. *Ibn Ḥawḳal, **BGA**, II, p.248; **Collection**, XXXVIII, p.97.*

40. *J. Laurent, **L'Arménie**, p.41; **BGA**, V, p.297.*

41. *Movsēs Dasxuranc'i , **History of Albania**, pp.126, 128, 130.*

42. *al-Iṣṭakhrī, **BGA**, I, p.183; Ibn-Faḳih, **BGA**, V, p.296; J. Laurent, **L'Arménie**, p.39.*

43. *Al Muḳaddasī, **BGA**, III, p.379; **Collection**, XXXVIII, pp.14-15.*

44. *J. Laurent, **L'Arménie**, p.44; W. Heyd, **Histoire du Commerce du Levant**, I, pp.44-45; M. Attaliates, **Historia, CSHB**, p.148.*

45. *Georgius Cedrenus, **Compendium historiarum, CSHB**, p.577; cf. J. Laurent, **L'Arménie**, p.44.*

46. *Aristakēs Lastiverc'i, **History**, (Erevan, 1971).*

47. *S. Der Nersessian, **Aght'amar – church of the Holy Cross** (Cambridge, Mass., 1965); also 'Armenia in the Tenth and Eleventh Centuries', **XIIIth International Congress of Byzantine Studies** (Oxford, 1967), pp.427-31.*

48. *Asołik, **Universal History**, pp.173-176.*

49. *Aristakēs Lastiverc'i, **History**, p.79.*

50. ***Ibid.**, XII, pp. 79-80.*

51. *Asołik in his **History** preserves a very interesting account of such an attack. In A.D. 980 a group of unknown individuals attacked the storehouse and granaries of the king and 'set them on fire', p.245.*

52. *Matthew of Edessa (Matt'ēos Uṙhayc'i), **Chronography** (Vałaršapat, 1898), pp. 153-154.*

53. *Aristakēs Lastiverc'i, **History**, XIV, p.89.*

54. *Matthew of Edessa, **Chronography**, p.103.*

55. *Yovhannēs Drasxanakertc'i, **History**, pp.258-259.*

56. *Aristakēs Lastiverc'i, **History**, XII, XXIV, pp. 80; 167.*

57. *S. Der Nersessian, 'Armenia in the Tenth and Eleventh Centuries', in **Byzantine and Armenian Studies**, Vol.I, p.326.*

58. *E. Lipshits, **Ocherki istorii vizantiiskago obshchestva i kultury VIII-pervaia polovina IX veka** (Moscow-Leningrad, 1961); S. Melik'-Baxšyan, **Armenia in VII-IX Centuries** (Erevan, 1968); D. Angelov, **Bogomilstvo v Bolgarii** (Moscow,*

1954); Max Beer, ***Social struggles in the Middle Ages*** *(Boston, 1924); B. Primov* ***Medieval Bulgaria and the dualistic heresies in Western Europe*** *(Sofia, 1960); W. H. C. Frend, 'Winning of the Countryside',* ***JEH****, XVIII, 1 (1967).*

59. *A. P. Evans, 'Social aspects of medieval heresy' in* ***Persecution and Liberty, Essays in Honor of G. L. Burr*** *(N.Y., 1931); M. Becker, 'Florentine politics and the diffusion of Heresy in the Trecento: A Socio-economic enquiry',* ***Speculum****, XXXV, (1959).*

NOTES TO CHAPTER IV
(pp. 37 - 46)

1. *F. C. Conybeare,* ***The Key of Truth, A manual of the Paulicians*** *(Oxford, 1898) (hereafter* ***KT****), lix - lx; Aristakēs Lastiverc'i,* ***History****, XXIII; Grigor Magistros,* ***Letter to the T'ulaili****, Kostaneanc' ed. (Alexandropol, 1910) (hereafter T'ulaili) p.164. Grigor Magistros, 'Syrian Kat'olikos',* ***BL****, p.158.*
2. *Grigor of Narek, 'Letter to the Abbot of Kčaw',* ***BL*** *XCII, pp.498-502, transl. in* ***KT****, appendix I, pp.125-130; Nerses Šnorhali,* ***Encyclical Letters*** *(Jerusalem, 1871), p.269.*
3. *Asołik,* ***Universal History****, (St. Petersburg, 1885), p.160. Conybeare makes the suggestion that the Lord Yovhannēs in question may be Yovhannēs Ōjnec'i,* ***KT****, lxii, n.1. The suggestion is wrong. 330 years separate Yovhannēs Ōjnec'i from Grigor Magistros and we should expect some reference to Smbat the sectarian in the works of Yovhannēs if they were contemporaries.*
4. *Grigor Magistros, 'Syrian Kat'ołikos',* ***BL****, pp.153-154.*
5. ***Ibid.****, p.167 ; cf. p.154.*
6. *Grigor Magistros,* ***Letters****, p.65; cf.* ***KT*** *appendix III, p.151.*
7. *The list of patriarchs starting from Grigor Magistros's time backwards is as follows: 1. Petros Getadarj (1019-1036-38-54), 2. Dioskoros (1036-1037), 3. Sargis (992-1016), 4. Xač'ik I (973-991), 5. Step'annos III (969-972), 6. Vahan (967-969), 7. Anania I (943-967), 8. Ełiše (938-943), 9. T'ēodoros I (932-938), 10. Step'annos II (931-932), 11. Yovhannēs V (899-931), 12. Zak-ariay I (855-877), 13. Yovhannēs IV of Ovayak (833-855), 14. David II (806-833).*
8. *Mxit'ar Ayrivanec'i,* ***History of Armenia*** *(Moscow, 1860), p.54.*
9. *G. Hovsepean,* ***Mxit'ar Ayrivanec'i, newly discovered inscriptions and texts*** *(Jerusalem, 1931), p.19 trans. [In Armenian].*
10. *Grigor of Narek, 'Letter to the Abbot of Kčaw',* ***BL****, XCIII, pp.498-502, transl. in* ***KT****, appendix I, pp.125-130; see M. Abełyan* ***Armenian Literature****, Vol.III (Erevan, 1968), pp.567-620. trans. [In Armenian].*
11. *Grigor of Narek,* ***BL****, pp.498-500; L. Arpee,* ***A History of Armenian Christianity*** *(Princeton, 1946), appendix I, pp.319-324.*
12. *Conybeare,* ***KT****, appendix I, p.126, n.3.*
13. *J. Markwart,* ***Südarmenien und die Tigrisquellen*** *(Wien, 1930), p.501.*
14. ***Digenes Akrites****, Introduction and commentary by J. Mavrogordato , ed., (Oxford, 1956), p.147.*

15. Π. Καρολιδης, Σημειωσεις κριτικαι ιστορικαι και τοπογραφικαι εις το μεσαιωνικον επος (Athens, 1906), p.242.

16. **Digenes Akrites**, p.146.

17. B. Sargisean, **Usumnasirut'iwn Manik'ea-pawłikean T'ondrakec'ineru ałandin ew G. Narekac'woy t'ułt'ê** (A study of the Manichaean Paulician sect of the T'ondrakec'i and the letter of Grigor of Narek)(Venice, 1893), pp.69-71.

18. A. Hovhannisyan, **Drvagner hay azatagrakan mtk'i patmut'yan** (Chapters from the history of the Armenian liberation movements)(Erevan, 1957), p.341.

19. S. P. Połosyan, **Gyułac'ineri čortac'umê ev gyułac'iakan šaržumnerê Hayastanum** (Serfdom and peasant movements in Armenia in 9-13th centuries) (Erevan, 1956), pp.367-370.

20. A. Ter Ghewondyan, **The Arab Emirates in Bagratid Armenia**, pp.52-53.

21. Constantine Porphyrogenitus, DAI, Vol.II, Commentary, pp.169-170.

22. M. Canard, 'Les H'amdanides et l'Arménie', **Annales de l'Institut d'études Orientales**, VII (1948), p.82;

23. F. C. Conybeare, **KT**, lxi-lxvii.

24. Samuel of Ani, **Collections**, p.91; Mxit'ar Ayrivanec'i, **History**, p.83.

25. R. Grousset, **Histoire**, pp.349-350.

26. Conybeare, **KT**, lxiii-lxiv; R. Grousset, **Histoire**, pp.350-351.

27. T'ovma Arcruni, **History of the Arcruni**, M. Brosset, trans. **CHA**, I, pp.101-102, **KT**, lxiii.

28. **KT**, lxvii; Grigor Magistros, 'Syrian Kat'ołikos', **BL**, p.153.

29. Sebēos, **History**, p.114; Step'annos Ōrbelean, **History of the province of Sisakan**, I, p.177; also **Histoire de la Siounie**, M. Brosset, trans. (St. Petersburg, 1884-1886), p.82, n.2.

30. Aristakēs Lastiverc'i, **History**, p.98.

31. Grigor Magistros, 'Syrian Kat'ołikos', **BL**, p.160. **KT**, appendix III, pp.147-148.

32. Grigor Magistros, 'Syrian Kat'ołikos', **KT**, appendix III, p.144.

33. S. Runciman, **The Medieval Manichee** (London, 1947); N. Garsoian, **The Paulician Heresy**, p.139.

34. E. G. Browne, **A literary history of Persia**, Vol.1 (London, 1919), pp.308-336; R. A. Nicholson, **A literary history of the Arabs** (Cambridge, 1930), pp.181-253.

35. *V. V. Barthold,* ***Encyclopaedia of Islam****, 2nd ed. arti. 'Abū-Muslim'.*

36. *V. Rosen,* ***Review of Sachau's edition of Al. Birunt's India*** *(St. Petersburg, 1889), p.156. See also G. E. Von Grunebaum,* ***Medieval Islam: A Study in Cultural Orientation*** *(Chicago, 1946), p.205f.*

37. *R. N. Frye, 'The Role of Abū - Muslim in the 'Abbāsid revolt'.* ***MW*** *(1974), pp. 28-38.* ***Encyclopaedia of Islam****, 2nd ed. article Abūl Muslim; R. Levy,* ***An Introduction to the Sociology of Islam****, vol. I, pp.35-36.*

38. ***Ałowank'*** *or* ***Ałwank'*** *in Arabic* ***Arrān al-Ran*** *corresponds approximately to present-day Soviet Azerbāyjān.*

39. *Yovhannēs Drasxanakertc'i,* ***History****, St. Martin, trans. (Paris, 1841), pp.145-146.*

40. *P. K. Hitti,* ***The Arabs in history****, p.103.*

41. *C. J. F. Dowsett, 'A neglected passage in the history of the Caucasian Albanians'* ***BSOAS****, XIX (1957), pp.456-468.*

42. *At the time of the Arab conquest, the mass of peasants were known by the semi-contemptuous term* ***'ulūj*** *("non-Arabs") – somewhat similar to the* ***raya*** *of the Ottoman Empire, see V. Minorsky,* ***Studies of Caucasian History*** *(London, 1953), p.112.*

43. *Quoted by I. Friedlander, 'The Heterodoxies of the Shiites in the presentation of Jon Hazm'.* ***JAOS****, XXVIII (1907), pp.1-80 particularly pp.35-37. A similar approach is taken by B. Lewis: 'It is more difficult to speak of any social or economic programme though their activities – and such successes as they managed to achieve – are clearly related to social and economic discontent, antagonism'., see B. Lewis 'On the Revolutions in Early Islam',* ***Studia Islamica****, XXXII (1970-1971), pp.215-231, and 'Some observations on the significance of heresy in the history of Islam' –* ***Studia Islamica****, I-IV (1953-55), pp.43-63.*

44. *V. Minorsky, 'Caucasica IV',* ***BSOAS****, XV (1953), p.509.*

45. *V. Minorsky, 'Caucasica IV',* ***BSOAS****, XV (1953), pp.504-529.*

46. ***Ibid.****, p.509.*

47. *bàtriqs = patricians.*

48. *V. Minorsky, 'Caucasica IV',* ***BSOAS****, XV (1953), pp.504-529.*

49. *Bābak himself had lived in Amaras after his defeat. Amaras is a village in the province of Arc'ax.*

50. *A. Ter Ghewondyan,* ***The Arab Emirates****, pp.37-38.*

51. *Movsēs Dasxuranc'i,* ***The history of Caucasian Albanians****, p.217.*

52. *al-Mas'ūdi VII, p.126 in J. Laurent,* ***L'Arménie****, p.113, n.10.*

53. *C. J. F. Dowsett, 'A neglected passage in the History of the Caucasian Albanians', **BSOAS**, XIX (1957), p.462.*

54. *Movsēs Dasxuranc'i, **ibid**, p.217; Irène Mélikoff, 'Notes Turco-Caucasiennes: Babek et Hurrani et Seyyid Battal', **BK**, XIII-XIV (1962), pp.72-81.*

55. *al-Mahdi mean literally "the guided one" and as all guidance (huda) is from Allah, it has come to mean the divinely guided one, guided, that is, in a peculiar and individual way. See the **Encycl. of Islam** (London, 1936), pp.111-115.*

56. *Grigor of Narek, 'Letter to the Abbot of Kčaw', **BL** XCII, pp.498-502; **KT**, appendix I, p.126.*

57. ***KT**, appendix p.128, n.6. Conybeare suggests that Iamres is 'a sobriquet for Smbat'. Iamres is the Armenian of Jannes and Jambres found in II Timothy 3 v.8. These names do not occur in the Old Testament, but extra-biblical allusions show that it is a reference to the Egyptian magician of Ex. 7-8, Jambres or Mambres (Mamre) from the Semitic root meaning 'to oppose'.*

58. *Grigor of Narek, 'Letter to the abbot of Kčaw', **BL**, XVII, pp.500-501, cf. **KT**, appendix I, p.128.*

59. *Grigor of Narek, **Ibid**, p.500.*

60. ***Ibid**, p.500.*

61. *Paul of Tarōn, Matenadaran MSS. no.5787, f.294b.*

62. *A. Hovhannisyan 'Dvizhenie Tondrakov v Armenii, IX-XIvv', **Voprosy Istorii**, X (1954), pp.100-108.*

63. *Grigor Magistros, 'Syrian Kat'oȟikos', **BL**, p.153; **KT**, appendix II, p.144.*

64. *Ališan, **Hayapatum** (Venice, 1901), p.550.*

65. *H. Ačaṙyan, **Hayaren Armataken Baṙaran** (Erevan, 1933), Vol.III.*

66. *Grigor Magistros, 'Syrian Kat'oȟikos', **KT**, appendix III, p.145.*

NOTES TO CHAPTER V
(pp. 47 - 54)

1. M. C'amč'ean, ***History of the Armenians from the Creation of the World to A. D. 1784 according to the accounts of all the sources***, *3 vols. (Venice, 1784-1786), II, p.884; B. Sargisian,* ***A study of the Manichaean-Paulician sect of the T'ondrakec'i***, *p.58; K. Ter Mkrttschian,* ***Die Paulikianer***, *p.85.*
2. *N. Garsoian,* ***The Paulician Heresy***, *p.139.*
3. ***Ibid***, *p.96.*
4. ***Ibid***, *p.146.*
5. ***Ibid***, *p.143.*
6. *A. Hovhannisyan, 'Dvizhennie Tondrakov v Armenii, IX-Xivv',* ***Voprosy Istorii***, *X (1956), pp.7-30; K. N.Yuzbašyan, 'K istorii Pavlikianskogo Dvizheneia v Vizantii v IXvv'. pp. 246-279; 'Tondrakskoe dvizhenie v Armenii i Pavlikiane', pp.31-44; A. Mnac'akanyan, 'T'ondrakyan šaržman mi k'ani glxavor harc'eri masin' (Some major problems of the T'ondrakec'i movement),* ***T***, *3(1954), p.63.*
7. ***Ibid***, *p.140.*
8. ***Ibid***, *p.140.*
9. ***Ibid***, *p.140.*
10. *Grigor Magistros,* ***Letters***, *K. Kostaneanc', ed. (Alexandrapol, 1910), p.164;* ***KT*** *appendix III, pp.141-151; V. Langlois, 'Grégoire Magistros',* ***CHAMA***, *I, pp.401-403.*
11. *Grigor Magistros,* ***Letters***, *p.168.*
12. *Grigor Magistros, 'Syrian Kat'ołikos',* ***BL***, *pp.158-159.*
13. *'Historia utilis et refutatio atque eversio haereseos Manichaeorum qui et Pauliciani dicuntur, Bulgariae archiepiscopo nuncupata,* ***PG***, *CIV, 1239-40; 1303-434.*
14. *Petrus Siculus,* ***Historia, PG***, *CIV, 1240-1241.*
15. *Photius Patriarcha, Codex Palatinus 216, in* ***PG***, *CII, 15-16; 83-84.*
16. *Georgius Monachus,* ***Chronicon***, *C. de Boor, ed. (Leipzig, 1904), II, pp.718-725.*
17. *Petrus Higumenus,* ***Appendix ad Petri Siculi historiam Manichaeorum seu Paulicianorum*** *(Göttingen, 1849); Petrus Siculus,* ***Historia, PG***, *CIV, 1253-54; Pseudo-Photius, 'Narratio de Manichaeis recens repullulantibus',* ***PG***, *CII, 23-24.*

18. N. Garsoïan, ***The Paulician Heresy***, *p.169 ff.*

19. *Grigor of Narek,* ***Book of Lamentations*** *(Venice, 1926), pp.477-492.*

20. ***Ibid***, *(Constantinople, 1850), p.221.*

21. *Grigor Magistros, 'Syrian Kat'ołikos',* ***BL***, *pp.158-159;* ***KT*** *appendix III, pp.143-149.*

22. ***Ibid***, *p.161 cf. S. Runciman,* ***Medieval Manichee***, *p.53, n.5.*

23. ***Ibid***, *p.161;* ***KT***, *appendix III, p.148.*

24. *Petrus Siculus,* ***Historia, PG***, *CIV,1253: Georgius Monachus,* ***Chronicon***, *p.721.*

25. *Grigor Magistros,* ***Letters***, *p.148, cf.* ***KT***, *appendix III, p.143.*

26. *V. Langlois, 'Mémoire sur la vie et les écrits du prince Grégoire Magistros',* ***JA***, *I, 6 série, XIII (1869), pp.5-64.*

27. *Grigor Magistros, 'Syrian Kat'ołikos',* ***KT***, *appendix III, p.149.*

28. *Grigor Magistros,* ***Letters***, *p. 162 cf.* ***KT***, *appendix III, pp.148-149.*

29. *K. Yuzbašyan, 'Paulician movement', pp.37-88; K. Ter Mkrttchian,* ***Die Paulikianer***, *p.89.*

30. *Petrus Siculus,* ***Historia, PG***, *CIV,1297-98B;* ***KT***, *p.148, n.5.*

31. *Georgius Monachus,* ***Chronicon***, *p.721.*

32. *Petrus Siculus,* ***Historia, PG***, *CIV,1297-98B, 1301-02A.*

33. *H. Grégoire, 'Pour l'histoire des églises pauliciennes καινοχώριον du Pont, Episparis en Φανάροια,'* ***OCP***, *XIII (1947), p.512 and 'Précisions géographiques et chronologiques sur les Pauliciens',* ***ARB-BL***, *5e série, XXXIII (1947), p.289 ff.*

34. *E. E. Lipshits, 'Voprosy Pavlikianskogo dvizheniia v osveshchenii sovremennoi burzhuaznoi istoriografii',* ***VV***, *V (1952), p.239.*

35. *Stephanus Diaconus,* ***Vita S. Stephani Junioris, PG***; *C. Halkin,* ***BHG***, *II, p.253; J. Gill, 'The life of St. Stephen the Younger by Stephen the Deacon; Debts and Loans',* ***OCP***, *VI (1940), pp.114-139.*

36. *Nikephoros Patriarch,* ***Antirrheticus, PG***, *C, 501B.*

37. *Theophanes,* ***Chronographia***, *I, p.501; Epistola ad Theophilum,* ***PG***, *XCV, 373B.*

38. *P. Charanis, 'Transfer of population as a policy in the Byzantine Empire',* ***Comparative Studies in Society and History***, *III (1961), pp. 140-154; 'Observations on the demography of the Byzantine Empire',* ***XIIIth International Congress of Byzantine Studies*** *(Oxford, 1967), pp. 1-19;* ***The Armenians in the Byzantine***

__Empire__ (Lisbon, 1969); 'Ethnic changes in the Byzantine Empire in the seventh century', __DOP__ XIII, (1959), pp. 25-36.

39. *Theophanes, __Chronographia__, I, p.429.*
40. *Nikephoros Patriarch, __Opuscula Historica__, C.de Boor, ed. (Leipzig, 1880), p.66 in __VV__, V (1952), pp.49-72.*
41. *Georgius Monachus, __Chronicon__, p.751.*
42. *Theophanes, __Chronographia__, p.501, see J. Martin, __A History of the Iconoclastic Controversy__ (London), p.157; L. W. Barnard, 'The Emperor cult and the origins of the Iconoclastic controversy', __B__, XLIII (1973). pp. 13-29; P. Brown, 'A Dark-age Crisis: Aspects of the Iconoclastic Controversy', __EHR__, 88 (1973).*
43. *Zigabenus, __Adversus bogomiles, PG__, CXXX, 1308.*
44. *Łewond, __History__, pp. 122-128; see Thorossian, __Littérature Arménienne__, pp. 108-109.*
45. *H. Bart'ikyan, 'Sources', pp. 88-92, __IANA__, VI (1957).*
46. *Theophanes, __Chronographia__, I, 488, cf. Georgius Cedrenus, __Historiarum Compendium__, I. Bekker, ed., __CSHB__, VI-VII (1838-39), II, p.39; N. Garsoian, __The Paulician Heresy__, p.123, n.42.*
47. *D. Obolensky, 'The Bogomils', __ECQ__, V (1945-46), p.153.*
48. *P. Lemerle, 'Thomas le Slav', __Travaux et Mémoires__ ,I(1966), pp.296-297.*
49. *E. Lipshits, __Ocherki istorii Vizantiiskogo obschchestva i kultury VIII pervoi polovina IX veka__ (Moscow-Leningrad, 1961), pp.213-228; 'Pavlikianskoe dvizhenie', __VV__, V (1952), p.68.*
50. *Theophanes, __Chronographia__, p.165.*
51. *__Ibid__, pp. 165-166; Le Strange, 'Al-Abrik, Tephrike, the capital of the Paulicians', __JRAS__ (1896), pp.933-941.*
52. *A. Vasiliev, __Byzantium and the Arabs. The political relations of Byzantium and the Arabs during the period of the Macedonian dynasty 867-959__, (St. Petersburg, 1902), pp. 25-26.*
53. *Theophanes Continuatus, __Chronographia__, pp.226-267.*
54. *A. Bryer, 'Excursus on Mananali, Samosata of Armenia and Paulician geography', __Iconoclasm: Papers given at the ninth symposium of Byzantine Studies__ (University of Birmingham, 1975), pp. 55-74.*
55. *N. Garsoïan, __The Paulician Heresy__, pp.139-140.*

NOTES TO CHAPTER VI
(pp. 55 - 72)

1. *Grigor Magistros, 'Syrian Kat'ołikos', **KT**, appendix III, pp. 143-44.*
2. *Grigor Magistros, 'Syrian Kat'ołikos', **KT**, appendix III, p.147.*
3. *Grigor of Narek, 'Letter to the Abbot of Kčaw', **BL**, XCII, pp. 498-502; **KT**, appendix I, pp.127-28.*
4. ***Ibid**, **KT**, appendix I, p.130. Cf. 'We learn from the same source that you ask, What writing directs any one to be anathematized? asserting the marvellously composed letter of contradiction of our blessed Lord Anania'. **KT**, appendix I, p.126.*
5. *Nersēs Šnorhali, **Encyclical Letters** (Jerusalem, 1871), pp. 333-400. **Sancti Nersetis Clajensis Armeniorum Catholici opera**, J. Cappelleti, Transl., 2 vols. (Venice, 1833), also in **KT**, appendix V, p.155.*
6. *'Gir Xostovanut'ean', Miaban (ed.) **Ararat**, (1892), pp. 5-18; H. C. Anasyan, **Haykakan Matenagitutyun** (Armenian Bibliography) (Erevan, 1959), pp. 530-40; 723-30.*
7. *K. Ter Mkrttschian, **Die Paulikianer**, pp. 83-84; B. Sargisean, **A study of the Manichaean-Paulician sect of the T'ondrakec'i**, pp. 108-17; E. Ter Minasyan, **Mijnadaryan axandneri**, pp. 151-53.*
8. *F. C. Conybeare, **KT**, appendix I, p.126, n.4; H. Bart'ikyan, **Sources**, p.141, n.27; M. Ōrmanian, **Azgapatum** (Constantinople, 191), vol.I, pp. 1144-45.*
9. *'Gir Xostovanut'ean, p.4.*
10. *Among these may have been Xosrov Anjevac'i, Grigor of Narek, and his uncle, the abbot Anania of Narek; C. J. Yarnley, 'The Armenian philhellenes: A study of the spread of Byzantine religious and cultural ideas among the Armenians in the X - XIth centuries A.D.', **ECR**, VIII, 1 (1976), pp. 45-53.*
11. *N. Garsoian, **The Paulician Heresy**, p.96; E. Ter Minasyan, **Mijnadaryan axandneri**, pp. 151-53.*
12. *Grigor of Narek, 'Letter to the Abbot of Kčaw', **BL**, pp. 498-502, in **KT**, appendix I, p.127.*
13. *Here the writer's malice must be discounted. This was the regular and stereotyped accusation against all heretics. It refers, of course, to the denial that marriage was a sacrament.*
14. *This is a reference to their rejection of the Armenian practice of offering of sacrifices for the dead, known as **matał**. Aristakēs Lastiverc'i, **History**, p.114.*

15. *The quotations are from the transl. of F. C. Conybeare, **KT**, appendix I, p.127; see also L. Arpee, **A history of Armenian Christianity from the beginning to our own time** (N.Y., 1946), pp.319-24.*

16. *Grigor of Narek, 'Letter to the Abbot of Kčaw', **KT**, appendix I, p.128. Smbat had been executed by the emir Aplvard. The reason is not known but the implication in the **Letter** of Grigor of Narek is that Smbat's claim to be a 'Christ' had been the cause of the attack.*

17-20. *Paul of Tarōn, in **KT**, appendix VIII, pp.176-76; Aristakēs Lastiverc'i. **History**, p.125; Grigor Magistros, 'Syrian Kat'ołikos', pp. 160-167; Nersēs Šnorhali **Letters**, p. 279; S. Der Nersessian, 'Une apologie des images du septième siècle', B, XVII (1944-45), p.71.*

21. *Grigor of Narek, 'Discourse concerning the Church against the Manichaeans who are Paulicians [sic]' in **Book of Lamentations** (Venice, 1926), pp. 477-92. In certain MSS. e.g. Matenadaran 1568, fol. 256, the name T'ondrakec'i is substituted for **Paulicians** in the title of the work.*

22. *Grigor of Narek, 'Letter to the Abbot of Kčaw', **KT**, appendix I, p.128.*

23. *Grigor Magistros, 'Concerning the representation of the holy church against the Manichaeans', **Letters**, p.168.*

24. *Grigor Magistros, 'Syrian Kat'ołikos', **KT**, appendix III, p.145; cf. Aristakēs Lastiverc'i, **History**, **KT**, appendix II, p.140 'Church and Church ordinances they utterly reject'.*

25. *Nersēs Šnorhali, **Letters**, p.269.*

26. *Paul of Tarōn in **KT**, appendix VIII, pp.176-76; Isaac **Kat'ołikos, Oratio I, PG**, CXXXII, pp.1179-82.*

27. *S. Der Nersessian, 'Image worship in Armenia and its opponents', **Armenian Quarterly**, I (1946), p.76; see **Armenian Byzantine Studies**, Vol.I (Louvain, 1973), pp.405-15.*

28. *Aristakēs Lastiverc'i, **History**, (Erevan, 1963), Chapters XXII–XXIII, pp. 119-133. See H. Thorossian, **Histoire de la Litterature Arménienne** (Paris, 1951), pp. 127-129, transl. **Histoire d'Arménie par A. Lastiverc'i**, by E. Prud'homme (Paris, 1864), F. C. Conybeare, **KT**, appendix II, pp. 131-140.*

29. *F. C. Conybeare, **ibid**, p.131.*

30. *F. C. Conybeare, **KT**, appendix II, pp.131-132.*

31. ***Ibid**, p. 132-133.*

32. *F. C. Conybeare, **KT**, appendix II, p.133-134.*

33. *F. C. Conybeare, **KT**, appendix II, p.134.*

34. *KT, appendix II, p.135. Kat'ołikos Sargis I Sevanc'i (992-1016). According to Aristakēs in 468 of the Armenian calendar (1019) he retired on account of old age and annointed Petros Getadarj (1016-1054).*

35. *Aristakēs Lastiverc'i, **History**, K. N.Yuzbašyan,ed., Chapter XXIII, pp. 125-33;', **KT**, appendix II, pp. 136-40.*

36. ***Ibid**, p.136.*

37. ***KT**, appendix II, p.136.*

38. ***Ibid**, p.137. These same allegations against the T'ondrakec'i are brought by Grigor of Narek in his 'Letter to the Abbot of Kčaw', **BL**, pp.499-500.*

39. ***KT**, appendix I, p.127, cf. **KT**, p.119.*

40. *Aristakēs Lastiverc'i, **History**, XXIII, p.98. See N. Garsoian, p.97, **KT**, appendix II, p.140. cf. Grigor of Narek, **Letter**, p.499; Paul of Tarōn, **KT**, p.176.*

41. *V. Langlois, 'Mémoire sur la vie et les écrits du prince Grégoire Magistros', **JA**, I, 6e serie, XIII (1869). pp.4-64.*

42. *Grigor Magistros, 'T'ulaili', pp.164-168, 'Syrian Kat'ołikos', transl. in **KT**, pp. 148-64; see Langlois, **Grégoire Magistros, CHAMA**, I, pp. 401-03.*

43. *Grigor Magistros, 'Syrian Kat'ołikos', **BL**, p.153; **KT**, appendix III, pp.143-9.*

44. *Grigor Magistros, **Letters**, Kostaneanc', ed., pp. 164-8; **KT**, appendix III, pp.141-51.*

45. *Grigor Magistros, 'T'ulaili', **KT**, appendix III, p.142. For the list of the 15 kat'ołikoi see Chapter IV, p.38, n.7.*

46. ***Ibid**, p.143.*

47. *Grigor Magistros, **Letters**, pp. 148-64. The full title of the letter is **The answer to the letter of the Kat'ołikos of the Syrians, at the time when he was dux in Vaspurakan and Taron, after the Manichaeans had been rooted out of the territory of the Greeks, and from T'ondrak, the remnant of this condemned race went to the Kat'ołikos of the Syrians in the city of Amid to try and win him over by their deceit.***

48. ***KT**, appendix III, 145.*

49. *Grigor Magistros, 'Syrian Kat'ołikos', 157; see **KT**, appendix III, 144.*

50. ***Ibid**, p.154, **KT**, appendix III, p.145.*

51. *Grigor of Narek, **Letter**, p.499; Paul of Taron, **KT**, p.176; Aristakēs Lastiverc'i **History**. See also **KT**, appendix II, p.140.*

52. *Regarding the two recanting heretical priests Grigor writes: 'They recounted to us word by word of their heresy, as it at present stands: for they knew their wicked and monstrous leaders accurately, and had been their attendants in their beastly, dirty hovels . . . '. Grigor defines the sect in the following manner – their preachings 'are represented in three separate forms. (a) To those who are more matured (or perfected) in wickedness, and are able to receive the deadly poison, they preach a sort of utter despair and godlessness, such as we find among Epicureans. But others (b) after the manner of Manichaeans whom they anathematize, at the same time they pursue the same practices. To others (c) they make a show of teaching in conformity with Christian tradition; yet they themselves make no confession at all, except what is repugnant to all Christian ordinances and beliefs'. Such groupings recall the obvious framework of the system of Valentinus (spiritual, physical, heathen, cf. I. Thess. V. 23) or the Manichaean classification: The Elect [Eklektoi], The Hearers and The Combatants. Grigor accentuates these traits by stating that the T'ondrakec'i said 'We are of the tribe of Aram, and agree with them in faith. But they in no way agree with us, but are much rather in opposition to us, and only resemble us in mere name as one dog does another. What comparison can there be where natures are so wholly different'. (**KT**, appendix II, p.147).*

53. *Grigor Magistros, 'Syrian Kat'oɫikos', **KT**, appendix III, p.148.*

54. *Grigor Magistros, 'Syrian Kat'oɫikos', p.161.*

55. ***Ibid, KT**, appendix III, p.148; Nersēs Šnorhali, **Encyclical Letters** (Jerusalem, 1871), pp.120-30. The Arewordik' should not be confused with the Paulicians, as was noted by K. Ter Mkrttschian, **Die Paulikianer**, p.103.*

56. ***Ibid**, p.148.*

57. *Grigor Magistros, 'Syrian Kat'oɫikos', p.162. Yuzbašyan **Paulician Movement**, 37-38 translates **Šnavank'** as 'the community of dogs', rather than the 'dog monastery' and takes this to be a reference to Peter of Sicily, **Historia**, pp.1297-8B. This is another punning explanation given by Grigor of the name **Koino-choritai** preserved by Peter of Sicily.*

58. *Grigor Magistros, 'Syrian Kat'oɫikos', p.154; **KT**, appendix III, p.149.*

59. *Grigor Magistros, **Letter** addressed to the deacon of the Kat'oɫikos Petros, p.35; Letter to a monk named Šaphu, p.134 in **Letters**, K. Kostaneanc' (ed.) (Alexandropol, 1910). Partial translation: **KT**, appendix III, pp.141-151.*

60. *Grigor Magistros, 'Concerning the representation of picturing of the church', **BL**, p.168; **KT**, appendix III, pp.149-50.*

61. *This accusation of Manichaeanism is made by Grigor Magistros and an explanation of the identification may be suggested, cf. 'Manichaeans . . . from T'ondrak' (**KT**, p.143), 'After the manner of Manichees . . . ' (p.147); '. . . derives from those Manichaeans who, having been utterly cut off from God, and having no hope of resurrection, are named T'ondrakec'i' (p.149). 'A column raised by the Manichaeans, i.e. the T'ondrakec'i', (p.151).*

62. *Grigor Magistros, 'T'ulaili', pp.167-8; 'Syrian Kat'ołikos', pp. 157-158, 162. He himself accuses King Gagik II of failing to put down the sect,* ***Letters****, p.269.*

63. *Melik-Set-Bek, 'Paul of Taron and the T'ondrakec'i',* ***Ējmiacin*** *IV (1960), pp.38-44; 'New sources on the T'ondrakec'i',* ***Aršav****, No.II (1940), pp. 51-4;* ***Georgian sources on Armenia and the Armenians****, 2 vols. (Erevan, 1936), p.122. (In Armenian). See* ***KT****, p.175.*

64. *The name Apellas may have derived from the Syrian* ***Abella*** *meaning monk (****Abeła****). It is not a reference to Apellas, Marcion's chief disciple as S. Runciman,* ***The Medieval Manichee****, suggests. It is the name of another T'ondrakec'i, heresiarch or follower unknown to previous writers.*

65. ***KT****, appendix VIII, p.175; S. Runciman,* ***The Medieval Manichee****, pp.60-61.*

66. *Matenadaran, Mss no.1154, f.240b; no.671, f.74b.*

67. *H. Bart'ikyan, 'Pavlikyanneri aṙaspelakan cagumê êst hin bułareren mi jeṙagri', (The legend of the origin of the Paulicians according to an ancient Bulgarian manuscript),* ***T****, 1 (1957), p.89.*

68. *K. Ter Mkrttschian,* ***Die Paulikianer****, p.80.*

69. *Nersēs Šnorhali,* ***Encyclical Letters*** *(Jerusalem, 1871; Ejmiacin, 1865), Latin translation by J. Cappelleti,* ***Sancti Nersetis Clajensis Opera****, 2 vols (Venice, 1833).*

70. *Grigor of Narek,* ***Letters****, p.499; Aristakēs Lastiverc'i,* ***History****, pp.120-121; Grigor Magistros, 'Concerning the Representation of the Holy Church against the Manichaeans',* ***Letters****, p.168; 'Syrian Kat'ołikos', p.157.*

71. *Nersēs Šnorhali,* ***Encyclical Letters****, pp.269-271.*

72. *Book containing the texts of the sacraments of the Armenian church.*

73. *Nersēs Šnorhali,* ***Encyclical Letters****, p.269. Cf. Paul of Taron, in* ***KT****, 175; Aristakēs Lastiverc'i,* ***History****, pp.119-20, also noted the abandonment of church buildings in the region overrun by the heretics.*

74. *Nersēs Šnorhali,* ***Encyclical Letter****, pp.275-83. See also E. Ter Minasyan,* ***The relation of the Armenian church with the Syrian church****, (Ējmiacin, 1908), pp. 260-3. [In Armenian].*

75. *Nersēs Šnorhali,* ***Letters****, pp.223-9, transl.* ***Epitres de Nerses le Gracieux*** *(Venice, 1839), pp.238-253; H. Bart'ikyan, 'Les Arewordi (Fils du Soleil) en Arménie et Mésopotamie et L'épître du Catholicos Nersès le Gracieux',* ***REA****, V (1968), pp.271-88.*

76. *H. Bart'ikyan, 'The answer of Grigor Magistros Pahlavuni to the kat'ołikos of Syria',* ***Palestinskii Sbornik****, No.VII (1962), pp.130-145, n.72-73, (Russian transl. of text with notes).*

77. *H. Bart'ikyan,* ***ibid****, p.139. See also* ***KT****, appendix II, p.148.*

78. *John of Ojun,* ***Contra Paulicianos****, (Venice, 1833), p.50.*

79. *The Book of Heresies,* ***Ararat*** *(1892), p.113.*

80. *H. Grégoire, 'Ο Διγενὴς 'Ακρίτας, 'Η Βυζαντινὴ ἐπ οποιια..' (New York, 1942), pp.202-12.*

81. *H. Bartikyan, 'Les Arewordi . . . ',* ***REA****, V (1968), p.273, n.5.*

82. *'Appendix monumentorum'. . . ,* ***PG*** *I, p.1465.*

83. *Nersēs Šnorhali,* ***Encyclical Letter****, p.223-9; H. Bart'ikyan, 'Les Arewordi en Armenie et Mesopotamie . . . '.* ***REA****, V (1968), pp.282-8.*

84. *Nersēs Šnorhali,* ***Encyclical Letter****, pp.223-9; H. Bart'ikyan, 'Les Arewordi en Arménie et Mésopotamie . . . ',* ***REA****, V (1968), pp.282-8.*

85. *Ełišē,* ***History of the Vartanians****, (Erevan, 1946); M. Ōrmanean,* ***The Church of Armenia****, G. M. Gregory, transl.(London, n.d.), p.28.*

86. *Amedroz, ed., (1908), p.264.*

87. *K. M. Setton,* ***A History of the Crusades****, (Philadelphia, 1958), Vol.I, pp.427-438.*

88. *H. A. R. Gibb,* ***The Damascus Chronicle of the Crusades extracted and translated from the Chronicles of Ibn-al-Qalanisi****, (London, 1932), p.247.*

89. *T. Avdalbekyan,* ***Anyayt ałandavorner Hayoc' mej 16-17 darerum*** *(Vienna, 1926) French trans. 'Sectes Armeniennes ignorees des XVIe et XVII siecles',* ***REA****, I (1964), pp.299-319.*

90. ***Xač'atur abełayi Jułayec'vo Patmutiwn Parsic'****, B. Ałavelian, ed. (Vałaršapat, 1905).*

91. ***Patmutiwn Parsic'****, p.115.*

92. ***Ibid****, p.115.*

93. *Grigor Magistros,* ***Letters****, pp.168-170.*

94. *Paul of Taron, **KT**, appendix VIII, p.175.*

95. *See appendix III.*

96. *H. Bart'ikyan, 'Concerning the evaluation of certain sources on the Paulician movement', **IANA**, VI (1957), pp.85-97.*

97. *S. Runciman, **Medieval Manichee**, p.46.*

98. *N. Garsoian, **The Paulician Heresy**, p.185 and n.165.*

99. *P. Lemerle, 'Histoire des Pauliciens d'Asie Mineure. Principales editions et etudes'. **Travaux et Mémoires**, V (1973), pp.12-15.*

100. *Cf. Aristakēs Lastiverc'i, **History**, pp.120-21; Gregory Magistros, **Letters**, p.168 'Syrian Kat'olikos', **Letters**, p.157.*

101. *Cf. N. Garsoian, **The Paulician Heresy**, pp.163-64.*

102. *F. Scheidweiler, 'Paulikianerprobleme', **BZ**, XLIII, (1950), pp.10-39, 366-84.*

103. *Aristakēs Lastiverc'i, **History**, **KT**, appendix II, p.140.*

104. *The term 'Transubstantiation' (not the concept) was first introduced not earlier than the first half of the eleventh century, and was defined as the official doctrine of the Catholic church during the pontificate of Pope Innocent III (1198-1216) at the Lateran Council of 1215, while the elaboration of the doctrine was not achieved till after the acceptance of the Aristotelian metaphysics later in the thirteenth century. See **Realenzyklopadie für protestantische theologie und Kirche**, (Leipzig, 1908), pp. 56-57. The point made on page 58 is also very relevant: 'This term and expression was adopted by the church in its controversy with the Albigensian and the Catharist sectarians; these sectarians were very similar to the T'ondrakec'i and perhaps influenced by them through the Bogomils. Since the 15th century the Eastern Church has used the word μετουσιώσις to denote an essentially identical doctrine and has on occasion given it formal approval, e.g. at the Synod of Jerusalem (1672); but many Orthodox theologians avoid the term, because of its close associations with Latin Scholasticism.*

105. ***KT**, Chapter XXII, pp.38-47, translation, pp.101-10.*

106. *The Gospel of Matthew, XVIII, 18; John, XX, 23.*

107. *N. Garsoian, **The Paulician Heresy**, p.163.*

108. *Such obscure expressions of the Armenian sources as, 'their self-conferred contemptible priesthood' (Grigor of Narek), and 'their outlandish election by consent' (Grigor Magistros), are best explained by accepting that some sort of recognised principle of government existed in the T'ondrakec'i church.*

NOTES TO CHAPTER VII
(pp. 73 - 83)

1. *Aristakēs Lastiverc'i,* ***History****, pp.79-80.*
2. *Matthew of Edessa,* ***Chronicle****, p.103.*
3. *K. Kostaneanc',* ***Annals on stones****, pp.5-6, 13.*
4. *Asołik,* ***History****, pp. 173-77 gives a detailed account of the monastic building activities. Matthew of Edessa,* ***Chronography****, (Vałaršapat, 1898), pp.48-9 and Samuel of Ani,* ***Collections from the writings of Historians****, p.104, gives the number of 115 for early eleventh century. Step'annos Ōrbelean,* ***History of the province of Siwnik'****, pp.426-27 gives 'more than 150'. There is no doubt that this is the number of the more famous religious institutions. A remark of Samuel of Ani, 'some say 900 monasteries' in Vaspurakan and Ōrbelean 'these are the number of the most famous monasteries; . . . but there are numerous others which I have not listed' confirms this.*
5. ***Liber Canonum of Armenians****, I, p.412.*
6. ***Annals on Stones****, p.1; Step'annos Ōrbelean,* ***History****, pp.179-180.*
7. *Matenadaran, Mss. no. 3031, ff.46-50.*
8. *X. Xafardaryan,* ***The monastery of Sanahin and its inscriptions*** *(Erevan, 1957), p.189. [In Armenian].*
9. *Yovhannēs Draasxanakertc'i,* ***History****, p.258-259.*
10. *Anania Mokac'i, 'Concerning the revolt in the house of Caucasian Albanians',* ***Ararat*** *(1897), p.132.*
11. *Grigor Magistros,* ***Letters****, p.154;* ***KT****, appendix III, p.144.*
12. *Step'annos Ōrbelean,* ***History****, pp.304-305.*
13. *Matenadaran, Mss. no. 3239, f.136a.*
14. ***Ibid****, Mss. no. 8075, f.159a.*
15. *Aristakēs Lastiverc'i,* ***History****, p.144;* ***KT****, appendix II, p.132.*
16. *V. K. Č'aloyan, 'The problem of a rennaissance in Armenia',* ***Sovetakan Graka-nut'yun ev arvest****, III (1951), p.139; see also* ***The Armenian Renaissance****, (Erevan, 1964), pp.57-63. [in Armenian].*
17. *S. Połosyan,* ***Serfdom and peasant movements in Armenia from the 9th-13th centuries.***
18. ***Ibid****, p.137.*
19. *N. Garsoian, 'Byzantine Heresy, a reinterpretation',* ***DOP****, XXXV (1971), p.89 ff.*

20. *N. Garsoian, 'Byzantine Heresy, a reinterpretation',* ***DOP****,XXXV(1971),p.89 ff.*

21. *Aristakēs Lastiverc'i,* ***History****, ch.XXII-XXIII.*

22. *S. Runciman,* ***The Medieval Manichee****, pp.30-31.*

23. *S. Runciman,* ***The Medieval Manichee****, p.132.*

24. *Petrus Siculus,* ***Historia, PG****, CIV, 1280-1281d.*

25. *N. Garsoian,* ***The Paulician Heresy****, p.30; pp.125-129.*

26. *D. Obolensky,* ***The Bogomils****, pp.168, 173, appendix IV; S. Runciman,* ***The Medieval Manichee****, pp.100-115.*

27. *Grigor Magistros,* ***Letters, KT****, appendix III, p.145.*

28. ***Ibid****, p.65,* ***KT****, appendix III, p.151.*

29. *Grigor Magistros,* ***Letters****, p.157;* ***KT****, appendix III, p.146.*

30. ***Ibid****, p.167;* ***KT****, appendix III, p.143.*

31. *A. Mnac'akanyan, 'Some major problems of the T'ondrakec'i movement',* ***IANA****, III (1954), pp.63-84. [In Armenian].*

32. *Grigor Magistros,* ***Letters****, p.162;* ***KT****, appendix III, p.148.*

33. ***Ibid****, p.167;* ***KT****, appendix III, p.146.*

34. ***KT****, appendix III, p.146.*

35. *Aristakēs Lastiverc'i,* ***History, KT****, appendix II, p.132.*

36. *Grigor of Narek, 'Letter to the Abbot of Kčaw',* ***KT****, appendix I, p.126.*

37. *Grigor Magistros,* ***Letters****, pp.167-168;* ***KT****, appendix III, p.143. A. Mnac'akanyan in his article: 'Some major problems of the T'ondrakec'i movement',* ***IANA****, III (1954), pp.63-84 has stressed the political activities of the T'ondrakec'i against the annexation of Armenia by Byzantium. On the basis of the theory that Grigor Magistros was a pro-Byzantine who served for the success of 'the Byzantine expansionist policy'. The T'ondrakec'i were therefore persecuted by Grigor Magistros because they objected to the annexation. However, since the publication of the above article, the premise of the above conclusion has been conclusively disproved. H. Bart'ikyan, 'On the question of Grigory Magistros' political orientation' and A. Mnac'akanyan 'Following the traces of Grigor Magistros' hymn',* ***Hayrenik'i Jayn****, 34 (1968), has shown that Grigor Magistros was never a pro-Byzantinist and did not favour the annexation of the Armenian kingdom of the Bagratid to Byzantium.*

38. *Grigor Magistros,* ***Letters****, p.152;* ***KT****, appendix III, p.143.*

NOTES TO APPENDIX II
(pp. 87 - 88)

1. *F. Cumont, 'La date et le lieu de la naissance d'Euthymios Zigabenus',* ***BZ****, XII (1903), pp.582-84, identifies Euthymius of Acmonia with Euthymius Zigabenus, who was entrusted by Alexius Comnenus with the task of composing a general refutation of all heresies, including that of the Bogomils. Ficker however, pp.182-91, has convincingly proved that Cumont's theory is untenable. The main argument against this identification is the chronological one: Euthymius Zigabenus wrote his* ***Panoplia Dogmatica*** *around 1110, while Euthymius of Acmonia could not have been born after 1000.*

2. *Ficker, alleging that there is no evidence that the Phundagiagitae ever begged, denies their connection with 'funda' and claims that their name must be derived from some unknown non-Greek root. Obolensky refutes this statement by remarking that this derivation exists in Bulgarian as well as in Greek; the name* ***torbeshi****, given in the Middle Ages to the Bogomils, is derived from the Bulgarian* ***torba*** *meaning a bag. See* ***The Bogomils****, p.178, n.1; D. Gress-Wright, 'Bogomilism in Constantinople',* ***B****, XLVII (1977), 163-185 suggests that the term 'Phundagiagitae can be derived from that of an old Islamic dualist sect, the Fida'i'.*

3. *N. Akinean, 'The Phundagiagitae', a review of G. Ficker's* ***Die Phundagiagiten****, HA, (1911), pp.763-65.*

4. *G. Ficker (Ed.): Die Phundagiagiten:* ***Ein Beitrag zur Ketzergeschichte des byzantinischen Mittelaters****, (Leipzig, 1908). See also his article 'Phundagiagiten' in* ***Religion in Geschichte und Gegenwart****, IV, pp. 1581-82.*

5. *G. Ficker,* ***Ibid****, pp. 66-68.*

6. *G. Ficker, 'Phundagiagiten' in* ***Religion in Geschichte und Gegenwart****, IV, pp. 40, 76, 33, 74.*

7. *M. Jugie, 'Phoundagiagites et Bogomiles', ÉO XII (1909), pp. 257-62; D. Obolensky,* ***The Bogomils****, pp.174-83.*

NOTES TO APPENDIX III
(pp. 89 - 97)

1. *BM, 5 (1960), pp. 333-344.*
2. *Alexander Eric'ian, 'T'ondrakec'i Armenians of our day', **P'orj** (Tiflis, 1880), pp. 102-103. (In Armenian).*
3. *Alexander Eric'ian, **Ibid**, p.108.*
4. ***Ibid**, pp.112-113.*
5. *A. Eric'ian, **Ibid**, p.114.*
6. *B. Sargisean, **A Study of the sect of the Manichaean-Paulician T'ondrakec'i, and the epistle of Grigor of Narek**, p.99, cf. K. Ter Mkrttschian, 'The Paulician and T'ondrakec'i sects in the light of Contemporary Criticism', **Ararat** (July, 1900), p.331. (In Armenian).*
7. *K. Ter Mkrttschian, 'Die Thondrakier in unseren Tagen', **ZKG**, XVI (1896), pp. 253-76.*
8. ***The Key of Truth: A manual of the Paulician Church of Armenia**, (Oxford, 1898).*
9. ***KT**, p.xxxi.*
10. ***Ibid**, pp.ixii-ixiii.*
11. *N. Garsoian, **The Paulician Heresy**, p.108.*
12. *N. Garsoian, **op.cit.**, p.108, cf. Arnold Toynbee, **Constantine Porphyrogenitus and his world**, (Oxford, 1973), p.671.*
13. *F. Macler, Review, in **RHR**, XLIV (1901), p.456.*
14. *M. Meillet, Review, in **Revue Critique d'histoire et de littérature**, N.S. XLVI (1898), p.169.*
15. *Guardian, Vol. LIII (12 Oct. 1898), pt.II.*
16. *N. Bonwetsch, see, **Realenzyclopädie für protestantische Theologie und Kirche- 'Paulikianer'**, p.53.*
17. ***KT**, p.xxxi.*
18. *Thorossian, **Littérature Arménienne**, pp. 192-193.*
19. *M. Abełyan, **History of Ancient Armenian Literature**, p.499.*
20. *Matenadaran, 'Archives of the Religious Synod', f.97, **Letter 133**, cf. A Eric'-ian, 'T'ondrakec'i in our day', p.115.*
21. *Matenadaran, Mss. no. 4481, f.297a.*

22. *Paul Meherian's manuscript is preserved in the Library of San Lazzaro (Venice).*

23. *B. Sargisean, **A Study of the sect**, p.102.*

24. *KT, p.lxxii.*

25. *B. Sargisean, **A Study of the sect**, p.103.*

26. ***Ibid**, p.103.*

27. *Matenadaran, Mss no. 4483, f.26.*

28. *Matenadaran, Mss no. 4483, f.226; cf. 'Archives of the Synod', **Letter** 6, document 164, p.2a.*

29. ***Ibid**, Mss no. 4481, f.395b.*

30. ***Ibid**, Mss no. 4483, f. 27b-28a.*

31. *Matenadaran, Mss no. 4483, f.27b-28a.*

32. *National Archives of Armenian S.S.R. Synod 1838, no.9, p.726b; cf. A. Eric'ian, **op. cit.**, p.108.*

33. *Matenadaran, 'Archives of the Synod', Document 133, f.5a; and A. Eric'ian, **op.cit.**, p.101.*

34. *A. Eric'ian, **The T'ondrakec'i**, p.109.*

35. ***Ibid**, p.109.*

36. *Matenadaran, Mss no. 6710, f.2a and 576.*

37. *Matenadaran, Mss no.4501, f.401a.*

BIBLIOGRAPHY

I. ORIGINAL SOURCES

a. GREEK SOURCES:

Abjuration Formula	Paulician Formula in 'Eine Sammlung von Abschwörungsformeln', G. Ficker (ed.) *ZKG*, XXVII (1906), 453-55. See also ***Travaux et Mémoires***, II (1970), 185-207.
Anna Comnena	***Alexiade***, B. Leib., (ed.) III Vols (Paris, 1937-45). Trans. by E. R. A. Sewter (London, 1969).
Cedrenus Georgius	***Historiarum compendium***, I. Bekker, (ed.) ***CSHB***, VI-VII (1838-39).
Constantine Porphyrogenitus	***De Administrando Imperio***, Gy. Moravcsik, transl. into English by R. J. H. Jenkins (ed.) (Budapest, 1949), II. ***Commentary***, R. J. H. Jenkins, (ed.) (London, 1962).
Digenes Akrìtes	J. Mavrogordato, (ed. and transl.) (Oxford, 1956).
Euthymius Zigabenus	***Panoplia dogmatica, PG***, CXXX, 1189-1244.
Georgius Monachus (Hamartolus)	***Chronicon***, C. *de Boor,(ed.),*(Leipzig, 1904), Vol.II.
Georgius Monachus (Continuatus)	***Vitae recentiorum***, *I. Bekker, (ed.),* ***CSHB***, *XLI (1838), 763-924.*
St. John Damascene	***Adversus Nestorianorum haeresim, PG***, XCV, 186-7; 223-24.
Michael Attaliates	***Historia***, Hase (ed.), ***CSHB*** (Bonn, 1853).
Nicetas Choniates	***Historia***, I. Bekker (ed.), ***CSHB***, (Bonn, 1835).
Petrus Higumenus	*Appendix ad Petri Siculi historiam Manichaeorum seu Paulicianorum,* ***Travaux et Mémoires***, IV (1970), 69-97.
Petrus Siculus	*Historia utilis et refutatio atque eversio haereseos Manichaeorum qui et Pauliciani dicuntur, Bulgariae archiepiscopo nuncupata,* ***Travaux et Mémoires*** IV (1970), 1-67.
Photius Patriarcha	*Narratio de Manichaeis recens repullulantibus,* ***Travaux et Mémoires***, IV (1970), 100-73.
Theophanes Confessor	***Chronographia***, C. de Boor (ed.), 2 Vols (Leipzig, 1883-85).

Theophanes Continuatus — ***Chronographia***, I.Bekker (ed.), ***CSHB***, XLI (1838).

b. ARMENIAN SOURCES

Agat'angełos — ***History*** (Venice, 1930), trans: 'Histoire du règne de Tirdate et de la prédication de St. Grégoire l'Illuminateur', ***CHAMA***, I, 105-194.

Anania of Narek — ***Confession of Faith***, Miaban (ed.) (Vałaršapat, 1892).

Aristakēs of Lastivert (Lastiverc'i) — ***History***, 3rd ed. (Venice, 1901). Transl. by M. Canard H. Berberian ***Récit des malheurs de la nation arménienne*** (Bruxelles, 1973).

Asołik — ***Universal History*** (St. Petersburg, 1885), transl. by E. Dulaurier, ***Étienne Asoghig de Daron, Histoire Universelle, première partie*** (Paris, 1883).
The Book of Letters (Tiflis, 1901).

Council of Dvin, A.D.554 — 'Oath of Union', K. Ter Mkrttschian (ed.), ***Ararat***, July, 1900.

Council of Šahapivan — Canons, in ***The Book of Armenian Canons***, A. Łlčean (ed.), (Tiflis, 1913). Transl. in N. Garsoian, ***The Paulican Heresy***.

Ełišē Vardapet — ***History of the Vardanians*** (Erevan, 1964) transl. by V. Langlois, 'Histoire de Varden et de la guerre des Arméniens'. ***CHAMA***, II.

Grigor Magistros — ***Letters***, K. Konstaneanc' (ed.) (Alexandrapol, 1910). Partial transl.in ***KT***, appendix III, 141-151.

Grigor of Narek (Narekac'i) — 'Letter of the Most Blessed Grigor Narekaci which he wrote to the magnificent and admirable congregation of Kčaw concerning the refutation of the accursed T'ondrakians', ***BL***, XCII, 498-502, transl. in ***KT***, appendix I, 125-130 and L. Arpee, ***A history of Armenian Christianity***, appendix I, 319-324.

John of Ōjun (Yovhannēs Ōjnec'i) — 'Oratio Synodalis', ***Opera***, J. B. Aucher (ed. and transl.), (Venice, 1834).

——— 'Contra Paulicianos', ***Opera***, J. B. Aucher (ed. and transl.) (Venice, 1834).

——— 'Contra Phantasiasticos', ***Opera***, J. B. Aucher (ed. and transl.), (Venice, 1834). English trans. in L. Arpee, ***A history of Armenian Christianity***, appendix II, 325-354.

______________ Canones, *Opera*, J. B. Aucher (ed. and transl.) (Venice, 1834).

John V. Drasxanakertc'i — *History*, (Jerusalem, 1867), transl. by J. Saint-Martin, *Histoire d'Arménie par le Patriarche Jean VI dit Jean Catholicos* (Paris, 1841).

John Mayragomeci (Yovhannes) — 'Letter to David bishop of Mec Kołmank', in Movsēs Dasxuranc'i, *History of the Albanians*, K. P. Patkanian (ed. and transl.), (St. Petersburg, 1861).

The Key of Truth — *The Key of Truth: A manual of the Paulician church of Armenia*. The Armenian text, F. C. Conybeare (ed. and transl.), (Oxford, 1898).

Kirakos of Ganjak (Ganjakec'i) — *Universal History*, (Venice, 1865), M. Brosset, *Histoire d'Arménie*, transl.(St. Petersburg, 1870).

Łewond (Ghevond) — *History* (St. Petersburg, 1887). Chahnazarian, *Histoire des guerres et des conquêtes des Arabes en Arménie par Ghevond*, (Paris, 1856).

Matthew of Edessa (Mattēos Uṙhaec'i) — *History*, (Jerusalem, 1869), E. Dulaurier, *Chronique de Matthieu d'Edesse* (962-1136), transl.(Paris, 1858).

Mxit'ar of Ayrivank (Ayrivanec'i) — *History*, J. B. Emin (ed.) (Moscow, 1860). transl. M. Brosset, *Histoire Chronologique par Mkit'ar d'Airivank' XIIIe S.* ,(St. Petersburg, 1869).

Movsēs Dasxuranc'i — *The History of the Caucasian Albanians by Movsēs Dasxuranc'i*, C. J. F. Dowsett (ed. and transl.) (London, 1961).

Nersēs II Kat'ołikos — 'Answer to the Letter of the Syrians from Nersēs kat'ołikos of the Armenians and Meršapuh bishop of the Mamikonean', *BL*, XI, 55-58.

Nersēs IV Šnorhali (Clajensis) — *Encyclical Letters* (Jerusalem, 1871), transl. J. Cappelletti, *Sancti Nersetis Clajensis Armeniorum Catholici, Opera*, 2 Vols.(Venice, 1833).

Paul of Taron — Matenadaran Mss.5767. Partial trans. *KT*, appendix VIII, 174-177.

Samuel of Ani — *Collections from the writings of historians*, A. Tēr Mik'alean (ed.) (Vałaršapat, 1893), M. Brosset, transl. 'Tables Chronologiques', *CHA*, II.

Sebēos — *Histoire d'Héraclius par l'évêque Sebèos*, F. Macler (ed. and transl.) (Paris, 1904).

Step'annos Ōrbēlean — *History of the province of Sisakan*, K. Šahnazarean, (ed.), 2 Vols. (Paris, 1859), M. Brosset transl., *Histoire de la Siounie* (St. Petersburg, 1884-86).

T'ovma Arcruni — *History* (Constantinople, 1852), M. Brosset, transl. *Histoire des Ardzrouni, CHA* I.

Xosrov Anjevac'i — Matenadaran, Mss. 8075.

Vrt'anēs K'ertoł — "Traîté contre les iconoclastes", S. Der Nersessian, in 'Une apologie des images au septième siècle', *B*, XVII, (1944-45), 58-69.

c. ARABIC, SYRIAN AND PERSIAN SOURCES

Bar Hebraeus — *The Chronography of Gregory Abul Faraj*, transl. E. A. W. Budge (Oxford, 1932).

al-Balādhurī — *The book of conquests of nations* (Baku, 1972).

Dionysius I of Tell-Mahrē — *Chronique*, transl. J. B. Chabot (Bibliothèque de L'École des Hautes Études, fasc.112, (Paris, 1895).

Ibn al-Athīr — *Histoire universelle* in A. A. Vasiliev, *Byzance et les Arabes, la dynastie d'Amorium* (Bruxelles, 1935), 349-69.

Ibn Khaldūn — *The Muqaddimah. An introduction to History*, F. Rosenthal, transl. (N.Y., 1958).

Ali al-Mas'ūdī — *Le livre de l'avertissement et de la revision*, B. Carra de Vaux, transl. (Paris, 1896).

Michael the Syrian — *Chronique de Michel le Syrien patriarch jacobite d'Antioche (1166-1199)*, J. B. Chabot, transl. (Paris, 1900-05).

al-Ṭabarī — *Chronique de Abou-Djafar-Mohammed-ben-Djarir-ben-Yezid*, H. Zotenburg transl., 4 Vols. (Paris, 1864-74).

——— *The reign of al-Mu'taṣim (833-842)*, transl. E. Marin, American Oriental Society, 1952.

d. ARABIC SOURCES

Ibn al Faqih, Ibn-Ḥawkal, Ibn-Khurradādhbih, al-Iṣṭakhrī, Qudāma (Kodama) are cited for the most part according to the edition of De Goeje, *Bibliotheca Geographorum Araborum* (Leyden, 1889).

II. MODERN WORKS

Abełyan, M. *Hayoc' hin grakanut'yan Patmut'yun* (History of Ancient Armenian Literature) (Erevan, 1944-1946).

Ačaṙyan, H. *Hayerēn armatakan baṙaran*, 7 Vols (Erevan, 1926-1935).

Adontz, N. *Armenia in the Period of Justinian. The Political Conditions based on the naxarar system*, transl. with partial revisions, N. G. Garsoïan (Lisbon, 1970).

Alexander, P. J. 'An ascetic sect of Iconoclasts in seventh century Armenia', *Late Classical and Medieval Studies in Honor of Albert Mathias Friend, Jr.*, (Princeton,1955), 151-160.

Anderson, J. 'The campaign of Basil I against the Paulicians in 754 and 815', *Classical Review*, X (1896), 136-140.

Arpee, L. *A history of Armenian Christianity from the beginning to our time* (New York, 1946), 101-119.

Bart'ikyan, H. 'K voprosu o Pavlikianskom dvizhenii v pervoi polovine VIIIv', *VV*, VIII (1956), 127-131.

——— 'Pavlikyan šaržman mi k'ani ałbyurneri gnahatman šurǰ', (Concerning the evaluation of certain sources on the Paulician movement), *T*, VI (1957), 85-97.

——— 'Pavlikyan hamayk'i kazmakerput'yan harc'i šurǰ', (On the question of the organisation of the Paulician community), *PBH*, III (1958), 183-187.

——— 'Pavlikyanneri aṙaspelakan cagumē ēst hin Bułarerēn mi jeṙagri', (The legendary origin of the Paulicians according to a Bulgarian manuscript), *T*, I (1957), 83-92.

——— 'Pavlikyan šaržumē Hayastanum VII-IX darerum', (The Paulician movement in Armenia in the VII-IX centuries), in *Hay žołovrdi patmut'yun* (Erevan, 1984), vol.2, pp. 389-415.

——— 'Armyanskie istochniki dlya izucheniya istorii Pavlikianskogo dvizheniya', (Armenian sources for the study of the Paulician movement), *Palestinskiĭ Sbornik*, IV (1959), 133-146.

——— 'Otvetnoe poslanie Grigoriya Magistra Pakhlavuni Siriĭskomu katolikosu', (The answer of Grigor Magistros Pahlavuni to the catholicos of Syria), *Palestinskiĭ Sbornik*, VII (1962), 130-145.

Bart'ikyan, H. 'Byuzandakan "Digenis Akritas" vipergut'yunē ev nra nšanakut'yunē hayagitut'yan hamar', (The Byzantine epic Digenes Akrites and its significance for Armenian studies), *PBH*, III (1963), 185-194.

——— 'Eshe raz o proisxozhdenii imeni "Pavlikiane" ' (Once again on the origin of the name "Paulician"), *IANA*, II (1973), 85-90.

Browne, E. G. *A literary history of Persia, Vol.I* (London, 1919).

Charanis, P. 'Ethnic changes in the Byzantine Empire in the seventh century', *DOP*, XIII (1959), 25-44.

——— *The Armenians in the Byzantine Empire* (Lisboa, 1963).

Conybeare, F. C. (ed.) *The Key of Truth. A manual of the Paulician Church in Armenia* (Oxford, 1898).

Cumont, F. 'La date et le lieu de la naissance d'Euthymios Zigabenos', *BZ*, XII (1905), 582.

Der Nersessian, S. 'Une apologie des images du septième siècle', *B*, XVII (1944-45), 58-87. Also in *Byzantine and Armenian Studies*, 2 Vols. (Louvain, 1973).

——— 'Image worship in Armenia and its opponents', *Armenian Quarterly*, I, I (1946), 67-81.

——— *Armenia and the Byzantine Empire* (Cambridge, Mass., 1947).

——— 'Armenia in the X-XIth centuries', *Proceedings of the XIIIth International Congress of Byzantine Studies, Oxford* (1967), 427-431.

Ficker, G. 'Eine Sammlung von Abschwörungsformeln', *ZKG*, XVII (1906), 443-464.

Garsoian, N. G. *The Paulician heresy: A study of the origin and development of Paulicianism in Armenia and the Eastern provinces of the Byzantine Empire* (The Hague, 1967).

——— 'Byzantine heresy, A reinterpretation', *DOP*, XXV (1971) 87-113.

Ghazarian, M. *Armenien unter der arabischen Herrschaft bis zur Entstehung des Bagratidenreiches. Nach arabischen und armenischen Quellen* (Marburg, 1903)

Gouillard, J. — 'L'heresie dans l'empire byzantin des origines au XIIe siecle', *Travaux et Mémoires*, I (1965), 299-324.

Grégoire, H. — 'Autour des Pauliciens', *B*, XI (1936), 620-614.

———— 'Les Pauliciens et l'iconoclasme', *Mélanges Cumont*, (Bruxelles, 1936).

———— 'Pour l'histoire des églises pauliciennes Καινοχώριον du Pont, Episparis en Φανάροια', *OCP*, XIII (1947), 509 ff.

———— 'Précisions géographiques et chronologiques sur les Pauliciens', *ARB–BL*, 5e série, XXXIII (1947), 289 ff.

———— 'Sur l'histoire des Pauliciens', *ARB–BL*, 5e série, XXII, (1936).

Grousset, R. — *Histoire de l'Arménie des origines* à *1071* (Paris, 1947).

Hakobyan, S. E. — *Hay gyułac'iut'yan patmut'yun (Vał feodalizmi darašrǰan)* (A history of Armenian peasantry in the early feudal period) (Erevan, 1957).

Hamazaspyan, V. — 'T'ondrakec'ineri šaržman ēpoxan ev gałap'araxosut'-yunē ' (The epoch of the T'ondrakian movement and their ideology), *IANA*, III (1949), 37-66.

Heyd, W. — *Histoire du commerce du Levant au Moyen Age*, 2 Vols. (Leipzig, 1936).

Hitti, P. — *History of the Arabs*, (London, 1949).

Hovhannisyan, A. G. — 'Dvizhenii Tondrakitov v Armenii, IX-XIvv', (The T'ondrakian movement in Armenia, IX-XIth centuries), *Voprosi Istorii*, X (1954), 100-108.

———— 'Smbat Zarehavanc'in, nra žamanakn u žamanakakakic'-nerē ' (Smbat Zarehawanc'i, his times and his contemporaries), *BM*, III (1956), 7-30.

———— *Drvagner hay azatagrakan mtk'i patmut'yan* (Chapters from the history of Armenian freedom movements) (Erevan, 1957).

Kaegi, W. E., Jr. — 'The Byzantine armies and iconoclasm', *BS*, XXVIII, (1968), 273-277.

———— 'al-Balā dhurī and the Armeniak Theme', *B*, XXXVIII, (1968), 273-277.

Kaegi, W. E., Jr. 'Patterns of political activity in the armies of the Byzantine Empire' in ***On Military Intervention***, ed. M. Janowitz (Rotterdam, 1971) [=***Papers of the Armed Forces and Society Group***, World Congress of Sociology, Varna, Bulgaria, 1970], pp.5-35.

——— 'Some perspectives on the Middle Byzantine period', ***Balkan Studies***, X (1969), 289-310.

Kremer, A. von ***Culturgeschichte des Orients unter den Chalifen***, 2 Vols. (Vienna, 1875-1877).

Langlois, V. 'Mémoire sur la vie et les écrits du prince Grégoire Magistros, duc de Mesopotamie, auteur arménien du XIe siècle', *JA*, I (1869), 1-64.

Laurent, J. ***L'Arménie entre Byzance et l'Islam*** (Paris, 1919).

Lemerle, P. 'L'Histoire des Pauliciens d'Asie Mineure d'apres les sources grecques', ***Travaux et Mémoires***, V (1973), 1-135

Leroy, M. 'Grégoire Magistros et les traductions arméniennes d'auteurs grecs', ***Annuaire de l'Institut de philologie et d'histoire orientale***, III (1935).

Le Strange, G. 'Al-Abrīk, Tephrikē, the capital of the Paulicians', ***JRAS***, (1896), 733-741.

Lipshits, E. E. 'Pavlikianskogo dvizheniīa v Vizantii v VIII i pervoi polovine IX vv.', (The Paulician movement in Byzantium in the VIIIth and the first half of the IXth centuries), ***VV***, V (1952), 49-72.

Lipshits, E. E. 'Voprosu Pavlikianskogo dvizheniia v osveshchenii sovremennoi burzhuaznoi istoriografi', (Problems of the Paulician movement in the light of contemporary bourgeois historiography), ***VV***, V (1952), 235-243.

Loos, M. 'Deux contributions à l'histoire des Pauliciens. I: A propos des sources grecques reflétant des Pauliciens', ***BS***, XVII (1956), 19-57.

——— 'Origine du nom des Pauliciens', ***BS***, XVIII (1957), 202-217.

Manandyan, H. A. ***K'nnaken tesut'yun Hay žołovrdi patmut'yan*** (A critical consideration of the History of the Armenians) (Erevan, 1945).

——— ***The trade and cities of Armenia in relation to ancient world trade***, transl. from the 2nd ed., N. G. Garsoian (Lisbon, 1965).

Mnac'akanyan, A. 'T'ondrakyan šaržman mi k'ani glxavor harc'eri masin' (Some major problems in the Tondrakian movement), *IANA*, III (1954), 63-84.

Maries, L. 'F. C. Conybeare (1956-1924) notice biographique et bibliographie critique', ***REA***, VI, 2(1926), 185-331.

Marr, N. ***Ani*** (Erevan, 1939).

Martin, E. J. ***A history of the Iconoclastic controversy*** (London, n.d).

Melik'-Baxšyan, S. ***Pavłikyan šaržumē Hayastunum*** (The Paulician movement in Armenia) (Erevan, 1953). Review article in *IANA*, X (1954), 87-95, by K.Yuzbašyan and H. Bart'ikyan.

——— 'Ditołut'yunner arabneri Hayastan katarac aṙaǰin aršavank'neri masin', (Observations on the first Arab invasions into Armenia), ***PBH***, 3 (1964), 79-90.

——— ***Hayastanê VII-IX darerum*** (Armenia in the VII-IXth centuries) (Erevan, 1968).

Miaban (G. Ter Mkrttschian) 'Girk' herjuacoc'', (Book of heresies), ***Ararat***, XXV (1892).

Minorsky, V. 'Caucasica IV: II. The Caucasian vassals of Marzuban in 344/955', ***BSOAS***, XV, 3 (1953), 504-529.

——— ***Studies in Caucasian History*** (London, 1953).

Morgan, J. de ***Histoire du peuple arménien*** (Paris, 1919).

Nalbandyan, H. 'Arabneri harkayin k'ałak'akanut'yunê Hayastanum', (The taxation policy of the Arabs in Armenia), ***IANA***, XII (1956), 73-84.

——— 'Arab ostikanerê Hayastanum', (Arab Ostikans in Armenia), ***T***, VIII (1958).

Nersoyan, T. 'The Paulicians', ***ECQ***, V, 12 (1944), 403-412.

Nicholson, R. A. ***A literary history of the Arabs*** (Cambridge, 1930).

Obolensky, D. ***The Bogomils: a study in Balkan Neo-Manichaeism*** (Cambridge, 1948).

——— ***The Byzantine Commonwealth, Eastern Europe, 500-1453*** (London, 1974), 163-166.

Ōrmanian, M. ***Azgapatum*** (National History), 3 vols. (Constantinople, 1914-1927).

Ostrogorsky, G. — *History of the Byzantine State* (Oxford, 1968).

Pōłosyan, S. B. — ***Gyułac'ineri čortac'umê ev gyułac'iakan šaržumnerê Hayastanum 9-13 darerum*** (The enslavement of the peasantry and peasant movements in Armenia in the 9-13th centuries) (Erevan, 1956).

Runciman, S. — ***The Medieval Manichee: A study of the Christian dualist heresy*** (Cambridge, 1948).

Sargisean, B. — ***Usumnasirut'iwn Manik'ēa-Pawłikean T'onrakec'ineru ałandin ew Gr. Narekac'woy t'ułt'e*** (Research on the Manichaeo-Paulician sect of the T'ondrakians and the letter of Grigor Narekac'i) (Venice, 1893).

Scheidweiler, F. — 'Paulikianerprobleme', ***BZ***, XLIII (1950), 10-39, 366-384.

Spuler, G. — ***The Muslim World*** (Leiden, 1960).

Starr, J. — 'An Eastern Christian sect: the Athinganoi', ***HTR***, XXIX 2 (1936), 93-106.

Stratos, A. N. — ***Byzantium in the seventh century***, Vol.1 (Amsterdam, 1968).

Ter-Łevondyan (Ghewondyan) Aram — ***The Arab emirates in Bagradid Armenia***. Transl. by N. G. Garsoïan (Lisbon, 1976).

Ter Minasyan, E. — ***Mijnadaryan ałandneri cagman ev zargac'man patmut'yunic'*** (From the history of the origin and development of sects in the middle ages) (Erevan, 1968).

Ter Mkrttschian, K. — ***Die Paulikianer im byzantinischen Kaiserreiche und verwandte ketzerische Erscheinungen in Armenien*** (Leipzig 1893). Armenian trans. (Jerusalem, 1938).

——— — 'Pavłikeanc' ew T'ondrakec'voc' ałandnerê ardi k'nnadatut'eamb', (The Paulician and T'ondrakian sects in the light of contemporary criticism), ***Ararat***, XXXIII (1900), 328-334.

Thomson, R. W. — 'The influence of their environment on the Armenians in exile in the eleventh century', ***Proceedings of the XIIIth International Congress of Byzantine Studies, Oxford*** (1967), 432-48.

Toumanoff, C. — ***Studies in Christian Caucasian History*** (Washington, D.C, 1963).

Toumanoff, C. 'The background to Manzikert', ***Proceedings of the XIIIth International Congress of Byzantine Studies, Oxford*** (1967), 411-426.

Toynbee, A. ***Constantine Porphyrogenitus and his world.*** Annex IV: 'The Paulicians and the Bogomils', (Oxford, 1973), 652-684.

Vaclav, M. 'Medieval heresy: gleanings and reflections' in ***Essays on the reconstruction of Medieval history***, Vaclav M. and Couse, ed. (London, 1974), 147-167.

Vasiliev, A. A. ***History of the Byzantine Empire*** (Madison, 1952).

Vryonis, S. 'Byzantium: The social basis of decline in the XIth Century', ***Greek, Roman and Byzantine Studies***, II (1959), 157-175.

——————— ***Byzantium: its internal history and relation with the Muslim world. Collected studies*** (London, 1971).

Wakefield, W. L. ***Heresies in the high Middle Ages*** (London, 1969).

——————— ***Heresy, Crusade and Inquisition in Southern France 1100-1250*** (London, 1974).

Xačikyan, L. ***P'ok'r Hayk'i soc'ialakan šaržumneri patmut'yunic'*** (The history of the social movements in Minor Hayk') (Erevan 1951).

Yuzbašyan, K. B. 'Tondrakitskoe dvizhenie v Armenii i Pavlikiane', (The T'ondrakian movement in Armenia and the Paulicians), ***IANA***, IX (1956), 31-44.

——————— 'De l'origine du nom "Pauliciens" ', ***REA***, IX (1972), 355-377.

——————— 'Fotii o proisxozhdenii imeni "Pavlikiane" ', (Photius on the origin of the name "Paulician"), ***IANA***, VIII (1973), 87-90.

——————— 'K istorii Pavlikianskogo dvizheniiâ v Vizantii v IX veke', (On the history of the Paulician movement in Byzantium in the IXth century), ***Voprosii istorii religii i ateizma***, IV, (1956), 246-279.

Zoryan, H. 'Arabneri harkayin k'ałak'akanut'yunê feodalakan Hayastanum' (The taxation policy of the Arabs in feudal Armenia), ***Erevani Petakan Hamalsarani Tełekagir***, II-III (1927).

INDEX

Note: Armenian names have been transliterated according to the Hübschmann-Meillet-Benveniste system. Arabic names are given according to the system of the *Encyclopedia of Islam*.